Perfect party games

Andrea
Campbell

Illustrated by
Sanford Hoffman

Sterling Publishing Co., Inc.
New York

793.2
Cam

Library of Congress Cataloging-in-Publication Data Available

1   3   5   7   9   10   8   6   4   2

Published by Sterling Publishing Company, Inc.
387 Park Avenue South, New York, N.Y. 10016
© 2001 by Andrea Campbell
Distributed in Canada by Sterling Publishing
℅ Canadian Manda Group, One Atlantic Avenue, Suite 105
Toronto, Ontario, Canada M6K 3E7
Distributed in Great Britain and Europe by Cassell PLC
Wellington House, 125 Strand, London WC2R 0BB, England
Distributed in Australia by Capricorn Link (Australia) Pty Ltd.
P.O Box 6651. Baulkham Hills, Business Centre, NSW 2153, Australia

Sterling ISBN 0-8069-2799-2

This book is dedicated to my women friends
Sue Brenneis, Elaine Warrington, Jill Aubry,
Judi Prestridge, and Ladonna Jackson,
for they give me encouragement, solace, and
an outlet for feminine understanding.

ACKNOWLEDGMENTS

Thanks goes out to all the groups who, over the years, have taken me in—from Beta Sigma Phi with their camaraderie, the Women's Club with their hundred-plus membership, to the Extension Homemaker's Club, a crafty kibitzy circle; the Pinochle crew; Village Writers; the Simian Society; and on and on. These are the individuals who have changed my life, along with the monkey children that some of them live with.

I'd also like to thank Sheila Anne Barry for her unflagging support. She wanted the book, sold the book to her colleagues, and worked on it as an editor—and friend.

Note to the Reader

The young have no problem with the carefree exuberance of congenial entertainment. Seniors have earned their poise from experience and have the time needed to savor life as they did in their youth. This book will serve both of these groups well, but the challenge is to arouse those in the long middle years, the ones in the hustle and struggle—the group least likely to find fun. Games encourage social intercourse and give back the free and easy amusement of youth. And for the overachievers in life, games help to keep faculties alive. With all the many types and kinds of parties I've thrown or have been a partner to, I have never had a poor time at a games party.

CONTENTS

INTRODUCTION

A celebrity once said that a good party begins in the kitchen and ends in the medicine cabinet. I don't agree with that one bit; neither food, alcohol, accidents, nor drugs should be the prime directive or result of any party. But I do believe the familiar is wholly unsatisfying. And this book means to stir up the familiar.

The best resource for any party is the people. If people weren't your principal concern, this book would be a primer on games for one (or games for two, if your spouse refers to others as "those people"). And there are games in here for everyone: the bold and the timid, the energetic and the laid back, the wicked and the merely mischievous. Most rely on the competitive element, a characteristic of child's play that is often bred out of adults—at least, at parties.

If you are not an aficionado of game-playing, don't worry. You will catch on and catch up to those of us who occupy the captain's seat—a most engaging place to be—and I wouldn't trade it for any other. Since you may not know me personally, I will tell you there are two things I hate: running late and not having control. If you are like me, you will be pleased to have purchased this book, because it keeps those elements in mind.

Also, if in the past you have felt much overwhelmed and trampled by party preparation—if, after all the cooking and carrying and the creating and arranging of sumptuous displays, you feel you have lost the enthusiasm for tackling games, this book is doubly for you. Because all that work is really secondary to having a good time. Of course, I'm not telling you *not to clean the house*—go ahead and do that and break out your best recipes—but just know that guests will not remember the cream-filled crusts as much as they will the rousing good time that was "had by all."

And finally, think about adding games into your traditional group events, such as the salon, the book club, and the cocktail party. Not only will playing games turn these events on their ear and make for unexpected interest, but other purposes will be achieved. For instance, in the salon I belonged to, some of our meetings would have been better had we played a few games to get to know each other quicker. We could have gotten into a subject without reintroductions each time. Games break down barriers.

I feel the same way about a book club, which can work smoothly much more quickly if the new members share a few games.

The same goes for a cocktail party. People who attend these parties usually fall into two groups. The first "works the room" and dominates the conversation. The second type never talks to anyone because they are reluctant to really mix, so they go home thinking they could have done better.

I wanted this book to show that games can work anywhere, bridging the gap between people meeting for the first time, and breaking down inhibitions rather quickly, so shared interests can come to light sooner—without all the secret, uncomfortable feelings people have about fitting in that come up a lot, whether people admit it or not. My foreign student exchange experience is a perfect example. The kids came to this country unwilling to speak out of fear of making a mistake or looking stupid (teenage angst, too). After playing games with other students and family members, the magic of hunts, the challenge of tests, and the interaction of tasks made them feel they had "lived through" a multilevel experience with the others, and bonded them instantly.

You can create this, too; master the magic.

HOW TO USE THIS BOOK

In the following pages are more than a hundred games for you to choose from for your next games-playing party or event. Before you begin, I suggest you develop a system. With a small investment in a file box and some 4" × 6" index cards, you will be able to organize your games by category for easy selection. When you file them, make a mark indicating the games you have played in the past, so that you can see at a glance the ones that you want to try out next time. This will be the beginning of your personal game file. Put the instructions for the game on one side of the card and the equipment or supplies needed on the other. Save some space at the bottom for personal notes—tips that you have discovered that will help you in the future. By adapting the games in various ways, you will learn what works best for you and your guests.

It's a good idea to have more activities or games planned than you will be able to use. That way, if something goes wrong, or doesn't turn out as planned, you can move quickly into another game without losing the enthusiasm you have worked so hard to build up. The important thing is to be flexible.

In addition to some terrific games, I am sharing many time-savers and charts that help speed me through my decisions. In the appendix you'll find the following checklists and planners:

Cleaning and Décor Checklist. You probably won't need—or even have time—to do all these things, but a checklist such as this will serve as both a time planner and a reminder of what to consider in order to ready the house for guests.

Types of Parties Checklist. This list will help you out when you're looking for an idea to exploit for either a particular month or occurrence, or when making up a social calendar. Also listed are some interesting themes that you might want to think about exploring.

Party Lifestyle Planner. While you may know exactly what kind of event you would like to stage, the lifestyle planner points out the different types of parties that will work with different age levels from 0–8 years of age to 75 and older. With it, you can be sure to choose a "just perfect" event when planning a party for others.

What to Do When. This week-by-week, day-by-day planner gives you a comprehensive breakdown of every step in the planning process, so that you can see where you're ahead, where you may be falling behind, and so that you don't miss any steps! An "at a glance" guideline, it is invaluable to me, and I think it will be of use to any savvy party planner.

I hope this book will be the first one you grab when you are thinking about hosting a party, event, or celebration. Make it your own, dog-ear your favorite pages, write in the margins, copy the templates, and have a go. A memorable party and a basketful of fun is yours for the making!

1.
THE SECRETS BEHIND GREAT GAMES PARTIES

I have always tried to hide my efforts and wished my works to have the light joyousness of springtime which never lets anyone suspect the labors it has cost me. —HENRI MATISSE

The *secrets* behind great games parties? Well, yes, there are hidden factors in this form of entertaining. It isn't that they're hidden for some clandestine motive or that the great hostesses won't share their secrets. It's because this kind of knowledge isn't evident unless you've experienced it. Plus, there's a lot to remember! And the best games-activity parties are the ones that run so effortlessly that guests don't notice the amount of preparation involved. The seamless choreography of events, balanced with time for food and camaraderie, is what party-givers strive for—an evening without a hitch.

This book is here to help you ferret out the necessary elements needed for great games and activities parties—the secrets, if you will—and the not-so-obvious details. Keep in mind that these suggestions are the nuts and bolts of using games for interactive parties. As you read, underline, highlight, and adapt the ideas to your own style. In fact, why don't you think about keeping a party journal? A special notebook or folder on your computer is a great place to
- keep track of guest lists and helpers
- evaluate locations
- make specific notes about facilities
- create templates for invitations
- log budget requirements
- record seating arrangements

and record a multitude of other data.

SECRET NUMBER ONE— GUEST AWARENESS

Dinner is ready . . . Guests will stall out of politeness. —UNKNOWN

The best host or hostess knows who the party is for—the guests—including the "honored guest," if there is one. Obviously, there are two main objectives:

- find the best way to make guests feel comfortable
- give them the best.

It's easy and very basic. In order to facilitate your guests' comfort and to break down the barrier that automatically exists when people enter a new domain, try to envision the event ahead of time, from your guests' point of view. Take each invitee into your mind and think about specifics. Does this special guest have allergies? Remember to keep those items away from them or off the menu. Vision problems? Make any writing clear and in large print. (We *all* need clear instructions.) Is one guest a diabetic? Provide food choices other than sweets.

Work at both perfecting greetings and making introductions. This all-important first contact sets the tone for your guests for the rest of the evening. And the best way to plan the beginning is to realize what the entrance to your festivity is like. Do a guest walk-through.

Pretend you are entering the house and follow the trail. Is there a coat rack? Will their wraps be easy to find? Can you accommodate a rainy coat or snowy boots? Is the guest bathroom accessible, outfitted with such niceties as tissues, fresh towels, and scented soap?

When the event is getting underway, try to be aware of an introduction that has not worked, a beginning that stalls or does not have the desired effect. If you see a non-mingler or someone who seems to be hiding behind a potted plant, fall back on a pre-party activity (see page 67).

And finally, while the event is running, have a ready ear to what's being said and a watchful eye to what's going on. It's up to you to monitor and take action when needed.

SECRET NUMBER TWO— GOOD CHEMISTRY

Unless you are entertaining a specific group, think diversity for your guest list. People with varied experiences and interests make for good conversation. If this is a gathering of familiar friends, introduce new faces. I once heard a hostess confess that she "casts her parties" as she would a play. I don't know how I'd feel about mixing poor students with rich lawyers, or Peter Pan with Captain Hook, but this formula works for her. Deciding whom to invite is an art unto itself. Spend some time with it.

In your journal, keep notes about your friends' interests and invite others they can play off of. For example, if your friend studies piano, he is likely to have something to say to a symphony conductor. There is one exception to this method: make sure that your guest list is not heavy with doctors, or all stockbrokers. This could not only lead to shop talk but it could make for one dull, dull evening. You want guests to leave the *office* mentality *at the office.*

The most obvious yet sometimes ignored advice is never to invite people you don't like. If you feel you have an obligation, satisfy it in another manner. If *you* do not like the person, why should you expect others to?

Also, it's important to understand group dynamics. You can mix the staid and pompous with the outrageous, the athletic with the studious, the well-read with the soap fans—just expect to have one heck of a brave evening! And don't let guests form into familiar cliques. Your seating arrangements, introductions, and games will go a long way toward avoiding the clustering problem.

And, finally, if the guest list is too long, have two different parties. What is too many? Plan around the space. If your party room is too large, tiny groups will hug the walls in cliques and refuse to enter blank space. Too small an area and your guests will not be able to move, get claustrophobic, and look for the exit. The ideal is a cozy gathering, where people can move but are still close enough to demonstrate near contact and relieve nervous energy—talking, happy, and eating. Twenty guests for lunch, for example, would allow you to chat with each one within a narrow time frame. Four people, and you might exhaust all avenues of conversation and suffer pregnant pauses.

SECRET NUMBER THREE—ATTITUDE

If some serious illness or unforeseen family disaster takes place, don't carry on. Your guests will not know how to respond appropriately and—let's face it—you won't be merry. But, barring those eventualities, put on a happy face. Parties are too much work to drop the ball as your first guest is pulling up the drive. Plan to have a great time! It's too late now to worry about the little things, and

there is an answer to the most needling problem that may come up. *Your attitude needs to be infectious.*

As adults, all of us have many responsibilities. Need I remind you, then, that parties are for having fun? Your mission is to encourage people to "climb out of themselves." It's okay to get a little silly, and people will not often get a chance to interact with others in the way they will under your guidance. Don't forget for a minute that your attitude will set the tone. Invited guests can't possibly think about taxes, troubles, or tribe if your theme is intact, your house smells wonderful, and they are met at the door by you or your most outgoing, synergistic friend.

Houses are simply settings, furniture merely things, and food comes in many forms, but guests are family and friends you care about.

SECRET NUMBER FOUR—OFFERINGS

As New York party planner Renny Reynolds—who has orchestrated more than 3,500 events—says: The essence of your event will come from your own personality, not from deep pockets. That said, what are "offerings"?

Offerings are about mood and atmosphere. Offerings are also the little unexpected touches that remind your guests that they're special. For mood setting, there are simple yet imaginative ways to transform your living room. To turn it into the deck of a ship for a Bon Voyage party, use an anchor, "Welcome Aboard" signs, and life preservers. A Mardi Gras party screams out for glittering masks, beaded necklaces, and jewels; a Graduation get-together needs mortarboard hats and scrolls; Valentine dinners suggest pink pillows, red hearts, and romantic music. Theme parties are interesting! A few well-placed props and construction paper can go far toward conveying another place or time. Pretend this setting is your theater, and you will be surprised at the amount of fun you can have realizing your ideas.

Pay particular attention to lighting and scents. Candle luminarias create a festive nighttime path while scotch pine and peppermint do a lot to conjure up childhood Christmas memories. Colored bulbs, strings of party lights, and disco balls can all affect the mood and character of your event. Just don't overdo. If you feel you have to monitor the candles, change the music, and jump up and down to collect hot oven treats, this "running ragged" will not add to conviviality. Your guests will silently groan as you depart the festivities for the fifth time.

For centerpieces and table settings, let your accomplishments and talents do the decorating. If you have beautiful garden surplus, make baskets of vegetables or bouquets of flowers for guests to take home. Do you pour candles, soaps, or make potpourri? Are you a seamstress or glue-gun aficionado? Create personalized placemats; put place cards in frames; have small baskets full of knickknacks, candy, and mementos. Then let guests take them home. These unexpected gifts are welcome surprises for your friends, and look at it this way: there'll be less to put away!

SECRET NUMBER FIVE—COOPERATION

Cooperation means setting both limits and expectations. By way of definition, cooperation is really two things: working or acting together, and being helpful and doing as you are asked.

What I mean by *limits and expectations* is that party givers should have a set of carefully thought-out "house rules." If you think about these key things beforehand, you can prevent almost any uncomfortable situation. Sometimes you may need to implement the rules with verbal instructions for all, a side comment to offenders, or with a look and a high sign, if they are family. Here are a few ideas:

Curfew. It is not unreasonable to expect people to have sitters and early morning appointments. And there can also be too much of a good thing! If you find yourself yawning and glancing at the late-night clock, you've not planned ahead. One of the best ways to dispatch hangers-on is simply to announce at your final game, "Why don't we play until 10:30 p.m. and then finish with dessert." People appreciate having a planned departure. If you absolutely feel you need help in this area, you can always take a vote. I believe guests do not want to overstay their welcome.

Smoking. The dividing line between smokers and nonsmokers is already clearly drawn. Personally, I do not allow smoking in my home because I am a nonsmoker and feel it is not healthy for me and others. For this reason, my friends and guests all know that they may exit to smoke on the deck outside or are free to use an area beyond the drive. You can forestall a problem by asking your smoking friends if they object to this arrangement when you issue the invitation. Knowing in advance that their smoking breaks need to be taken outside usually disposes of this issue. The simple truth is that today smokers can spoil an evening for nonsmokers. Don't let that happen.

Drinking. The best advice I've heard is never to rely on the consumption of alcohol to create a party atmosphere. For people with substance abuse problems, drinking can create exactly the opposite effect—a belligerent guest. While it is not your duty to mandate anyone else's lifestyle choices, it is up to you to make sure a guest does not leave your home driving drunk. In fact, in some states it is the law. Call a cab or a friend to drive them home.

Signals that a guest may have had too much are uncharacteristic behavior, mood swings, changes in posture, loud speech, lack of major motor skills, and inappropriate behavior.

There are several ways to deal with this situation. The first is simply to gauge the amount your guests have had to drink. After a certain proscribed limit, change to another beverage—coffee, Cokes, or tea. It's always wise to have plenty of alternatives, such as nonalcoholic mixes, specialty waters, juice, and soda.

The next best solution is just to stop at a certain hour. Say a designated cocktail hour ends at 7:00 p.m. From then on, you can serve food, games, and dessert to help your guests wind down. One famous hostess, K. Callan, suggests giving each drinker a pencil and paper for their signature every thirty minutes. She sets it up as a type of game but with serious overtones. Guests become witness to their own deterioration and incompetence, and this provides an awareness of the number of drinks they've consumed. She also recommends being on the lookout for the consumption of more than one drink per hour. Games hostesses will probably be too busy to be watchful, so a time limit seems most reasonable. You or your assistant can perform a presto-change-o by substituting other beverages for alcohol at an appointed hour.

Drugs. The first and most obvious solution is not to invite the offenders in the first place. But if you cannot ward off the problem in advance, discreetly and quickly escort them out. Let them leave through a side door and do not allow good-byes to the group. You are not a policeman, but you are responsible for your guests and their well-being while they are in your home. The important thing is not to feel intimidated by taking the hardline. Immediate action is needed in face of the presence of drugs.

Costumes. Certain festivities call for costumes. A formal fund-raising event, political do, or celebrity ball often requires ballroom or theme-related attire. And, occasionally, at a private function, such as a cocktail party, it is doubly fun to get dressed up. A party located on a dude ranch with hayrides and horses seems best when people can wear denim, riding boots, and Stetsons. It's your call, of course. But if anyone feels seriously uncomfortable with costumes or setups, don't push it. If they arrive in plain clothes, so be it. Unless they are painfully shy, by the end of the evening they may wish they'd gone the extra mile like the others.

Overnight. Any type of party can present an unexpected predicament. An out-of-town guest may have car trouble, someone may feel too wired, tired, or ill to drive, or a late arrival may have gotten lost. The gracious offer of overnight accommodations, or even arrangements at a nearby hotel, will make things a lot easier for those involved. Ahead of time, then, make sure the guest room is cleaned, the bed dressed with fresh sheets, and towels laid out. Complete the generosity extended to your guest by offering a morning breakfast prior to departure. Be prepared for all situations.

SECRET NUMBER SIX—ASSISTANTS

All games-party leaders know there is nothing as valuable to an event as capable assistants who can be cued in to help. Choose people who are efficient and polite, and who can exude confidence and enthusiasm.

Spend some time before the party explaining the overall game plan to your helpers. Delegate specific jobs, showing exactly what equipment and materials are to be used and letting them know when to hand them out. Write down any crucial details and advice if there are other duties you would like them to attend to, such as taking coats, extinguishing candles, removing props, chairs, or trash, or just lending a hand to what generally comes up. This pre-planning is integral and will not only establish the order of events but will also help to anticipate any flaws in your setup.

Game-wise, you can expect an assistant to hand out or fill in name tags, conduct a demonstration, distribute supplies, direct people into groups or formations, fill in for an odd number of players, act as a partner, change the music, or serve as judge or time-keeper. The fact that the assistants are *not actually playing* places them in an unbiased position and helps reinforce their standing as arbiters, official counters, or final decision-makers.

Make sure you delegate authority to your helper early on by introducing him or her to the group as *your helper,* someone they can look to for assistance. You might even want to prepare a special apron for your helper to wear. Sew or glue his/her name on it in large felt letters and make sure the apron has large pockets to accommodate little games pieces or even trash. That will take some of the heat off you while you are planning the next game, counting out supplies, or perhaps handling an unexpected disturbance.

If your event includes a mixture of children and adults, you might want to assign one "big" person for every three children. At a large party, you can ask friends to play host or hostess in various rooms or in different areas. Instead of relying on your friends or guests, you might even want to hire a couple of college students or someone from the drama department at your local university. Just don't have too many volunteers; that can become a problem.

By the way, I save a gift for each one of my assistants to thank them for their participation.

SECRET NUMBER SEVEN—TIMING

Timing is to a game-activities party what the beat is to a dance number. Don't plan to go forward without it! And there is so much to say about the importance and intricacies of timing that an entire book could be written about that alone. As I said in my first party book, *Great Games for Great Parties,* "Your advance planning will make all the difference in the flow of activities and how relaxed and confident you will be as a leader." With that in mind, let's hit the most important points about timing now, and we'll talk about timing guidelines again in later chapters.

Always have more games ready than you think you will need. Maybe a game moved faster than anticipated, the puzzle was solved early through a stroke of genius (or a lucky guess), or someone has ruined the fun. Make light of it by saying, "Boy, you players are brilliant! Why don't we try this . . . " And, that said, you can segue into the next planned venture. If you move swiftly, your guests won't have a chance to notice.

Don't ignore a player or team's winning. After all, if your guests have no incentive to play, their motivation will be dampened. Award a prize, let them bow, or just generally throw some attention their way.

Make it easy for people to wait on themselves. Sometimes it's easier to let team leaders collect the paper and pencils, game boards, or playing pieces rather than depending on your assistant to pass out 24 sets of material. Shortcuts to materials facilitate the flow.

Constantly assess a game's playing time. Either circulate or monitor the responses on the game-players' faces. (You can also do this behind a camera; just take photos as you watch.) If several players are chatting or looking at your dado molding, the game has gone on too long.

Seek to have overall balance and timing in your game plan. Perhaps your first activity is a pre-party game played by individuals, such as a contest or guessing game. Choose a second activity that gets everyone together as a group—maybe a game that puts people into groups of four. Then, using those groups, have a game that keeps that formation but is more active, in which they can work as a team. After that, a change of position is needed—a different formation or grouping. Small group games followed by team activities present good contrast.

Finally, the closing activity should bring the whole group back together just before refreshments. A climactic game will leave everyone happy and exhilarated. The food will leave them satisfied and content. If your guests are still eager to play after eating, you can introduce table games and the "brainier" type of activities.

SECRET NUMBER EIGHT—ZING!

Zing! is the pop-up "Jack" in the crank-spun box, the plot twist at the end of the movie, and the rainbow at the end of the storm. It's a pleasant surprise or an unexpected delight in an otherwise predictable setting.

Look for the Zing! factor for all your parties. You can achieve it through a clever use of theme that starts with the invitation. Maybe you have written the invitation on a balloon and the recipient must blow it up to discover the news. You might fill a plastic bag with sand for a beachside hangout and write the invitation particulars on a seashell or paper umbrella tucked inside. For Christmas, you could deliver your invitation on a decorated gingerbread man, attaching a tag, or if you're very patient, writing it in icing. You might even think about having the invitation delivered by a real person in costume, such as a cowboy who delivers the news about a "bang-up" country music awards party.

Zing! is also a comfortable house setup for a games-theme party.

Pull out all the stops when looking for props and the little touches that help to carry out the motif. Get ideas from specialty paper and party stores or women's magazines. Use your computer and crafting skills to create backdrops, photos, decorative placemats, personalized trinkets, and fantasy objects.

Zing! can also be created by the presentation of treats, drinks, and food. For a beautiful chilled treat, cut the top third off an empty half-gallon paper milk carton. Place a slender bottle of vodka or vodka and juice mixture on the inside, in the middle. Arrange a few flowers, orange slices, or greens between the carton and the bottle. Fill the carton with water and freeze. Just before serving time, tear off the "paper carton mold" to reveal your design within the ice block, all around the bottle. Voila—your own ice sculpture!

Zing! could be a surprise guest, entertainment, or interesting focal point. A twist for New Years? Maybe you can invite a Tarot reader to give everyone's forecast for the brand-new year. Your Zing! scheme can be as grand as the amount of time and money you're

willing to invest and is limited only by what you can imagine. Give it some time; stretch your mind; brainstorm with friends. Party planning and the anticipation of an event are half the fun.

And finally, Zing! is lots of gifts, clever prizes, theme favors, and mementos, and most of all, specially driven attention. Be willing to let your mind climb out of its straitjacket. Your guests will appreciate the care you take with details whether they remember to tell you or not. The creative pursuit lives within all of us.

To Recap:
- Keep a party journal.
- Visualize things from your guests' point of view.
- Spend time on your guest list.
- Practice meeting, greeting, and observing.
- Plan to have fun.
- Use theme, mood, and atmosphere.
- Have predetermined "house rules."
- Use assistance wisely.
- Pay particular attention to timing.
- Add Zing! however you can.

2.

FROM ROUGH DRAFT TO MASTER PLAN

Go out into the highways and hedges and compel them to come in,
that my house may be filled.   —BIBLE, LUKE 14:23

Opening our home allows us the freedom and ingenuity to share our bounty, personality, and talents with others outside of our family. By inviting outsiders in, we strengthen the commonality between us and share what we have earned from our work, in creature comforts and convenience. Without a periodic celebration of life, how can we realize what's been gained? Keep the big picture in mind and there will be less panic the first time you organize an event.

ADVANCE PLANNING

Advance planning provides the kind of backdrop that will give our guests a unique mixture of smooth presentation, gaiety, and charm. So with these ideas as our focus, we lead into the plan.

Think about preparation step-by-step. No seamstress making a dress or magician performing a trick would attempt their task without a pattern, practice, and plan. They know what the desired outcome should be, and so do you. In the beginning, the more you put on paper the less you have to rely on your memory. In addition, the better you control your time, the more you can concentrate on the fun, creative side of the pursuit, and the less you chance getting sidetracked by thinking of hospitality as drudgery. And finally, the better your advance planning, the better your party will be for everyone—you and your loved ones included.

PARTY TYPE

Calendar. The time of year can dictate events to celebrate, such as birthdays, anniversaries, and holidays. For instance: It's fall; you love hot spiced cider and colorful leaves, and would like to celebrate the change of season. Maybe you would like to have a Halloween party but don't want to get involved in costumes or dress-up. What else can you do to make it festive? Halloween parties have the theme pretty well lined out, but for an activity you could stage a team-driven pumpkin-carving contest. Too messy? Let your guests decorate orange balloons with colored markers!

In addition, guests could play a matching game using spooky objects. Say, for example, a spider needs some webbing, a witch needs her broom, a scarecrow needs his hat, etc. Cut these items out of cardboard or paper (or use the real thing) and distribute them around the room, taping them to walls, tables, chairs, drapes, and so on. Give each guest or couple some paper and a pencil and have them study the different objects posted and find the match. First one finished wins a prize from the coffin, or plucks one off the hanging ghost line (prizes draped with squares of white sheet—add eyes and O's for mouths and hang from a clothesline).

Remember to look through the other games listed in this book. You can adapt them in order to use the autumn or Halloween motif on props, words, and gimmicks. You might even want to cross one theme with another. For example, a Halloween party could become an NFL Halloween (based on a sport), a "Star Wars" Halloween (based on a movie and its characters), a Hawaii Halloween (based

on a location), a Fifties Halloween (based on a time), a Hoedown Halloween (based on an activity like a square dance).

By putting together these "interactive" theme-related activities and games, you can give a traditional party a new way to go. Any major holiday or celebration has the potential for twists. Get inspired by the original, and then make it your own!

Food. Once you've decided on the type of party that appeals to your current mood, budget, and sensibilities, it's time to define your idea further with food choices. Think about different ways to serve food:

Buffet	Casual
Breakfast or Brunch	Outdoor
Cocktails	Potluck
Formal Luncheon	Seated Dinner
Tea	Away Entertaining

Or a simpler version of these types, such as

Dessert sampler	Deli style
Wine and cheese	Grilling
Cookie exchange	Finger food
Salad bar	Snack food stations
Build-your-own (sundaes, pizzas, etc.)	

Make this decision and a large part of the planning has already begun!

Time. From the second week in November until after the first of the new year, people's schedules are very busy with required festivities related to career, school, or other family commitments. If you are set on having a party during this time, make it as easy as possible for people to attend by advising them well in advance. Also, think about making your party a less elaborate fete, with a limited time parameter, such as a Bunko party, which is an event based on dice-rolling with a mixing element in it. If you want your guests to meet everyone else, Bunko is fast and fun and may be the evening event for you. Be careful not to decide upon a party that requires extensive fussing, food preparation, or a myriad of details for you—or you might end up wishing you hadn't planned a party during this heavily scheduled time. Your no-show quota may be high.

STEP-BY-STEP

There are a lot of questions to answer when planning a party, but this is an exciting part of the process—building anticipation. Here's your chance to design whatever it is you hope to have happen and, given the lists and suggestions here, you can shape the choices so they are uniquely yours.

If you are entirely new to entertaining and feel unsure about what to do, opt for the easiest plan—next time you can be more adventuresome. No guest will be unhappy if you are a gracious person and have striven to put yourself and your friends at ease. Even the most lavish of affairs is a wash if the host is frazzled or on edge.

All parties that appear to be seamless have much thought and preparation behind them. And parties built on advance planning and work, if it's a happy pursuit, will be smooth because of your patient execution of the details.

PARTY JOURNAL BASICS

These are some of the factors that make up a party. Add or subtract categories as needed

- Type (or Theme)
- Purpose
- Guests (Honored Guest)
- Place (or Where)
- Date (or When)
- Time
- Invitations
- Menu (or Food)
- Décor
- Games and Activities
- Gifts, Favors, and Prizes
- Dress Options
- Special Considerations
- Seating Plan

To get a glimpse of the party-planning process take a look at the simple beginning scheme for a Newcomer Coffee on page 29. You could use it to welcome new neighbors into the community. The purpose is to help establish rapport for a continuing relationship.

By using this fundamental template (a blank form is in the back of this book for you to copy), you can begin thinking about almost any function. In addition, you can use your computer to design, reconfigure, and keep templates in party document files—easy to update. Of course, the more complex the plan, the more features you will need to incorporate into the design.

For example, you might want to:

- add the names of more guests
- elaborate on the menu selections
- note food preferences, allergies, or religious taboos

PARTY PLAN:

Type: Newcomer Coffee

Purpose: To meet new neighbors

No. of Guests: Four couples including:

Honored Guests: New couple and their two children (one children's helper)

Where: At home and on the deck

Date: Sept. 10, Sunday afternoon

Time: 2:00 p.m.

Invitation: Personal request, will call to see if still convenient

Food:
Oatmeal apple muffins
Cinnamon toast
Cookies

Coffee, tea, and punch
Fresh fruit
Chicken salad sandwich bite
Petite quiches

Décor: Place mats illustrating the new couple's home (a photo or computer image pasted on foam board and covered with clear contact or laminating sheet)

Games/Activities: Map of Treasure Isl., Area Quiz, City "Tour" Highlights, and a game with personal identification qualities

Gifts, Favors, Prizes: baskets filled with samples/coupons/bus. cards from area businesses

Special Considerations: Have a special table set for children near ours. Provide videotape of Walt Disney's "Aladdin," a puzzle, crayons, coloring book, and a cleared table area for children to work on in den (with popcorn? ask parents first). Jordan will supervise children; leave French doors open to deck.

- add theme or decorating notes
- use special music or a backdrop
- designate a particular set of dishes or serving pieces
- add the names of assistants, or phone numbers of the hired servers or caterers
- include special notes for surprise elements or things you want to remember.

These additional notes can all go on a master plan, or you might decide to build the party through a series of distinct checklists, marking them individually as you proceed, but keeping them all together. I like the idea of having some control over lists and keep mine in a slender 3-hole binder, checking things off as I go. Sometimes I highlight items that still need attention. Just make sure each list has a heading at the top, such as DECORATING CHECKLIST, so you know at a glance what you're looking at.

An added suggestion: sometime before the actual preparation of a meal, I'll leave small post-it notes at various places to help me remember things such as at what temperature a dish is to be reheated, the garnish I want to add, or a reminder to check the bathroom throughout the evening. This type of conscientious organization is still the best way to have and gain control over any planned event.

ENTERTAINING OPTIONS

Time-of-day appropriateness will determine what serving pieces to use, the kind of atmosphere you can achieve, and the accoutrements that are suitable. For example, candles are always festive, but obviously not a great choice on a luncheon table set in the hot sun. In planning, though, it helps to be aware of the standard times for meals:

Standard Times for Meals

Breakfast: before 11:00 a.m.   Cocktails: 6:00–8:00 p.m.
Brunch: 10:00–2:00 p.m.   Dinner: 7:00–9:00 p.m.
Lunch: 11:30–2:30 p.m.   Dessert: 9:00 p.m.–
Tea: 3:00–5:00 p.m.   Late supper: 10:00 p.m.–

These times may certainly be violated. If, for example, someone in the group you have invited for a dinner-games evening is a diabetic and coming straight from work, you wouldn't play games first and make him wait until 8:00 p.m. to eat, unless you offer quite a few substantial appetizers to hold him over. As with anything else, use your foreknowledge about guests and your good judgment, and you can tweak the schedule to fit your needs.

Don't be afraid to tinker with basic times either; there's something exciting about skewing the expected. Say, for example, that you know holiday plans and stresses are wearing down your women friends at work. You seem less burdened than the others, and you want to acknowledge them sometime during the winter festivities. They are willing, excited at the prospect of breaking away from family pressures, and they may also have gifts to exchange with each other. You might plan a special after-dinner tea, or even a late-evening brunch. You could serve a light repast of lovely cream-cheese-filled croissants or waffles with fresh fruit spreads made from frozen berries together with champagne.

A prerequisite could be that everyone "dress down"—or suggest that each woman bring along her bedroom slippers to snuggle into. Choose games that are especially humorous or that lend themselves to "women only" humor. Events that women plan for themselves and other busy women often make for the best and most rewarding times. Too often the seasonal stresses of celebrating traditional holidays are the responsibility of women who already work full-time. This is a nice way to blow off some holiday steam; a breakfast menu couldn't be easier to prepare, and the camaraderie of games makes a holiday in itself.

Don't use your heirlooms for a party or gathering. It's difficult to remain gracious about losing your great-grandmother's sugar bowl after one of your guests has dropped a spoon and chipped it. I believe in enjoying treasured items, but using important or valuable legacy pieces at a party is pushing the curve of hope.

Just a Note on Java

I have a particular preference about coffee: I like mine made from real beans, fresh, and very hot. I am not alone. After going to too many functions where the brew was inferior or, heaven forbid, instant—I implore you to use the best. For only a few dollars more you can sniff fine-smelling, freshly brewed coffee. Pay particular attention to the coffee-maker's suggestions and double-check the correct amount for large urns.

In addition, please surprise your guests and friends with real cream in nice pitchers and several types of sugar, either in cubes, packages, or bottles. Avoid using that powdery sugary stuff that coats spoons and clings to the bottom of the cup. For pizzazz, you might have cinnamon or peppermint sticks for stirrers.

And not everyone drinks coffee, so make tea drinkers happy with a nice assortment of flavors in addition to the regular kind; add a nice Orange Pekoe flavor, an Earl Grey, or a mellow, fruit-flavored blend.

Also make absolutely certain that the pot you begin with is sparkling clean, and use a clean, fresh filter so your brew will not be spoiled by a bitter bite. If you're uncertain about the quality of the water you're using, bring bottled water and avoid any mineral-heavy brands.

ESTIMATING COSTS

A simple formula to determine costs was suggested to me when I first started out. If you are not going to actually itemize expenditures as you go along, you can expect that half the money will be spent for food (50%), beverages will take one-quarter (25%), and the flowers, centerpiece, prizes, or extras will comprise the other fourth (25%).

I suggest you keep track of costs and list them in your party-planning notebook. Even if you think at the time you're too tired to deal with this, you may discover the party was such a success it bears repeating—with a different roster of guests perhaps—or maybe others will ask for help in planning their next event. So hang on to all receipts and act the wiser. In the future, even if you decide not to repeat the same party, at least you will have your notes on costs and can fall into the allocation pattern quicker.

FUND-SAVER TIPS

The biggest advantage to starting your entertaining plan early is that you'll save money because of it. There are, in fact, several ingredients involved in controlling costs.

Organizing

It's usually the last-minute dash to the convenience store, the deli, or the bakery that breaks the bank. Each item that you select on the run has a premium attached to it—you are paying for the convenience of someone else doing the work. All the rising, rolling, baking, and frosting are done for you. The appeal of roasted chicken and the honey-glazed slow-bake ham is obvious—they're complete. Generally, anything you make from scratch is bound to be less expensive than that. Even the stop at the 24-hour mart for batteries or extension cords is sure to cost you. And this is all right. It's good that you have the convenience of being able to buy these things quickly if you're pressed for time or are coping with a disaster. Just realize that a purchase of convenience will put a still bigger dent in your budget.

If, instead, you plan ahead and are not subject to last-minute pressure, you can shop at discount stores for appliances, supplies, and accoutrements. This way you will be able to buy in bulk and repackage the items when you get home, taking only what you need and storing the rest for later consumption.

One fund saver, if you're organized and plan far ahead, is haunting summer garage sales, antique shops, and the odd assortment of flea markets. Maybe the extra pitcher you need is there on the 50¢ table, or you might just stumble across an extra chair. Repaint or recover and voilà. You might even find stray pieces for serving, such as salt cellars, or a display item that you wouldn't want to pay department store prices for. Architectural graveyards are fun, too. Expect to find plaster pediments, old iron-gate fence pieces, and molding—all decorative and extremely hot for refashioning into screens, for wall art, and as stands for objects.

The major holidays are a good time to buy packaged sets of things. Maybe you'll discover a comb, brush, and hand mirror for your guest bathroom around Mother's Day, or a sundae kit with specially shaped goblets, an assortment of toppings, and an ice cream scoop left over from Valentine's and perfect for a prize!

Pick up ornaments, special papers, and ribbons on sale after Christmas. A golden cherub, a softly flossed reindeer, or expensive wired ribbon can be used at any time of the year, and the retailers practically give the stuff away after Christmas so they don't have to store it or ship it away a second time.

Shopping

Know your supermarket layout. The better you know the organizational web the grocer has set out for you, the less you will be snared into the wandering trap, a science developed by grocers and many other businesses. The goal is to entice you into walking through the entire store (that's why the milk is housed in the back). They hope that, when you come in, you are already hungry and can be lured into picking up packages of food that have drawing power. The theory behind this is obvious: a simple stop for milk and bread

will then net double-digits' worth of processed, prepared, or deli-type foods, which are more expensive. Think about it: for the same price you'd pay for a chunk chocolate surprise cake with chocolate curls on top, you could buy three cake mixes plus whipped cream toppings. To combat this, prepare a computer template of your own supermarket. Close your eyes and walk through the imaginary market in your mind, writing down just what lives where. (And unless your market has recently remodeled or moved its shelving, you'll probably be able to do this easily.) Soon you will have a map that tells you the canned vegetables and fruits are on aisle #2, baking products and staples are housed on aisle #4, and cleaning supplies are awaiting purchase on aisle #10. The result of this advance planning means that if you are short one or two items, you do not have to travel each aisle, and are not enticed into wasting more time than necessary. Like a hawk you can pinpoint your direction, select your needed purchase, and be queued up in the "less than 8 items" check-out line before you can say "Saved hassle."

Here are a few other tips to help you with shopping and buying:

- Make use of white sales for linen purchases
- Collect serving trays and invest in a good trolley or cart, plus buy a fold-down snack tray set
- Know your store personnel and services
- Don't shop when hungry
- Borrow unusual items, but be sure to return goods promptly in good, clean order, and if you need the item more than twice, buy it
- Barter or trade services—say, exchange a knitted cap (your forte, you have dozens!) for a floral arrangement
- Give yourself time to recuperate between shopping trips
- Make circle shopping trips, visiting geographically compat–ible areas

COOKING AND SERVING

Serve reasonably sized portions. I think the tendency in some restaurants today is to deliver a chef's salad in a family-sized serving bowl, an overblown sandwich fighting for space alongside coleslaw and a half bucket of fries, and an onion-ring blossom that could take care of a party of six. Realistically, most people do not realize what nutritionists mean when they talk about *an average serving*. Besides, if you use beautiful plates with reasonable portions and present a nice sampling of variety, texture, and color, you won't need gargantuan servings. When you pay special attention to the ambiance, details, aromas, and setting, guests will want to relax, and leisure helps make food more filling.

- Learn to create soup stocks and different bases. Almost every enticing entree is served with a sauce or in a decorative pool of base made with glaze or juice, herbs, and condiments. It is the delicate puddle of lemon sauce that makes a Grateful pudding; it is the tang and colors of dipping sauces that entice you to Tempura; and it is the Crème Anglaise that gives a dessert an exotic French touch. Try them.
- Use cloth and real fabrics that can be washed instead of paper products. Not only are they nicer to the touch, strong and durable, but they can be decorated, dyed, cut, resewn, and used again and again. Most landfill waste is paper products, so you'll also be helping the environment by decorating with linen.

CRAFTING

Think about making your own invitations using rubber stamps, any variety of papers, cardboard, and glue-on items. Use stencils or metallic pens. Your notes will look as good as the more expensive card-shop cards, and your creativeness will generate enthusiasm because your attention to detail announces right off—this party's going to be good!

- Pick and arrange flowers from your own garden. If you're not a gardener, buy two or three silk flowers or ornaments every time you shop over a two-month period and you will have a nice display by party time. Barring these suggestions, consider buying large flowering bushes from the local nursery. Separate the bushes into smaller plants with some trimming and repotting. Also, consider using annuals and herbs, which are usually no more than a dollar or so for starter trays.
- A wily planner uses fresh vegetables for decorations and centerpieces. And if you select vegetables from a farmer's market, or buy them direct from the farmer, you have the advantage of getting produce at the early stages of freshness. By the time the produce is at its peak, it can be served to your family after the party. That is, of course, unless you have gilded or painted the finish; then it's sacrificed to the gods of decoration.

To Recap:

Consider the calendar carefully.

- Tweak common holidays or events, by using double themes.
- Traditional parties need games or activities, too.
- Select food and preparation according to time, mood, and budget.
- Use a party journal and template to help define your needs.
- Post-it notes make great "helpers."
- Don't be afraid to tinker with basic times.
- Put away expensive heirlooms.
- Estimate party costs at 50% food, 25% beverages, and 25% other accoutrements.
- Get in the habit of keeping receipts.
- Record expenses in your party journal for reference.
- Convenience food is more costly; to save money, make things from scratch.
- Buy in bulk.
- Make your own invitations and flower or vegetable arrangements.
- Look for summer and holiday sales.
- Cut portion sizes; learn to create soups and bases.

3.
YOUR BEST FIRST TOOL: LISTS

To get something done a committee should consist of no more than three people, two of whom are absent. —ROBERT COPELAND

In order not to exhaust yourself with party details, plan ahead and keep lists. Not only does a list let you determine what needs to be done in the grand scope of things, but as you scratch off each item, you will feel a sense of satisfaction and can *see for yourself* that you are indeed getting things done!

The party is shaping up. By now, you have a pretty good idea of the special purpose or honored guest for your party. Some theme suggestions appeal to you and your mood, and you've started to think about how to implement related ideas. Your guest selection is firming up and you have visualized the event by running it through like a movie in your mind. You have begun to weigh the effort

involved and at least estimated in your head how much money you can comfortably spend.

Your best first tool for organizing all the details involved with entertaining is a Step-by-Step Planning Checklist. Start one a month or several weeks before the party and use it to assess your progress. A sample checklist is printed below.

STEP-BY-STEP PLANNING CHECKLIST

Pre-Party Planning

Step 1—Decide on the theme for the party. (Consult list of theme suggestions for ideas, if needed. See pages 46-47.)

Step 2—Purpose for, or honored guest?

Step 3—Fill out a Guest List.

Step 4—Invitations. Commercial, home-made, or specialized printing? If purchased, add to shopping list along with stamps.

Step 5—Assess room situations needed.

Step 6—Begin selecting games or activities.

Menu Planning

Step 1—Formulate your basic menu and consult recipes.

Step 2—Prepare grocery list; don't forget garnishes.

Step 3—Make a Sample Menu worksheet (and post-it notes with the temperature and time for each dish prepared).

Step 4—Note special items for purchase.

Bar Planning

Step 1—Do a bar inventory.

Step 2—Develop a liquor, wine, and beverage grocery checklist.

List of Party Chores

Step 1—Include tasks that require a longer time element—for example, things that require repair, painting, cleaning, and so on, and plan for services now.

Step 2—Make one list for days required to run errands, arrange rentals, etc.

Step 3—Create another list for days to work in the house.

Grocery Shopping

Step 1—Gather recipes, menu plan, coupons, notes, and draft a grocery list. Review each recipe one at a time so that you will purchase all supplies, in the correct amounts, and have all ingredients when you're ready to assemble.

Step 2—Group similar items together to make it easier to shop.
Step 3—Plan trip for supplies like candles, paperware, etc.

Cleaning

Step 1—Review your Cleaning List—a sample is included at the back of the book—and spread out heavy or complicated jobs over a series of days to avoid exhaustion.
Step 2—Add any needed cleaning supplies to your grocery list.

Cooking

Step 1—Each night review the recipes you plan to make the next day, allowing for special instructions, thawing, or preparation.
Step 2—Make and freeze as much as you can ahead of time.

Serving

Step 1—Inventory your serving pieces and plan your dishes accordingly.
Step 2—Plan bar and serving spaces. Draw simple diagrams of traffic patterns and test the convenience of your plan.
Step 3—Draw a buffet plan for food service; test them for fit.

Decorating

Step 1—Make a list of decorating supplies and plan your theme.
Step 2—Devise a list of what you have, what you need to rent or borrow, what you want to purchase.
Step 3—In the evenings, begin to assemble and craft artwork, baskets, or supplies.

Games and Activities

Step 1—Select your games, noting the amount of time needed, the space of the game, and make sure you have enough of a variety to keep it interesting. Copy them onto index cards for your convenience. Set up a Games List.
Step 2—Collect supplies, draw templates, score sheets, etc. Add sundry items to your shopping list.
Step 3—Assemble prizes, favors, and gifts. Wrap if necessary.
Step 4—Read over Leadership chapter.
Step 5—Line up assistants and list how they can help you: in greeting, distributing supplies, acting as photographer, etc.

Recordkeeping

Step 1—Make copies of all receipts, forms, and plans for your party journal.
Step 2—Start a Costs List.

GUEST LIST

Your Guest List worksheet should have the names and phone numbers of the guests, their mailing or e-mail addresses, the date you sent the invitation, and the date they responded (or the date you will phone to follow up). Do not assume anything and leave nothing to chance. If you are counting on someone's attendance, I suggest a telephone call follow-up.

TRAFFIC PATTERNS AND SETUPS

Now would be a good time to assess your space allowance and traffic patterns. Some games call for a lot of movement. Draw a simple plan of the room or rooms and try to visualize people moving around, playing the games. You may want to remove fussy plants, floor lamps, or any precious items. Check to make sure there are no cords strung across traffic areas; look for rugs that are not lying flat, or objects that might be knocked over when the room swells with people. Running around at the last minute, sweeping up plant dirt, or collecting things for storage during a party makes people feel anxious. It's best to be realistic about what should stay and what needs to be put away for party safety.

Will people need surfaces to write on, lights to see by, places to return used cups, a facility for trash? Take all this into consideration in your room plan. You may want to move the furniture now so you can get used to the arrangement and not trip over novel placements as you do the actual setup.

If you are using a buffet scheme for food service—which is almost always the best plan for game parties—you might want to draw up a plan of the table and decide where you are going to place each object. Then you can determine if this arrangement will facilitate the best traffic flow and make for easy "food on the fly." If your layout permits it, you might want to close the door to the dining area until the games-activity plan calls for food or refreshments.

GAMES BOX

Games usually require supplies. Instead of having to go through the house collecting materials each time I have a party, I have created a games box. It is a large plastic box with a lid that holds all the supplies needed for almost any game plan. Keep adding to your games box over time. Since all the materials will be in one place, you won't hesitate to use it whenever you can—for example, have a

game handy to pepper meetings while waiting for a group to assemble, or to add inspiration to a brainstorming.

Here is an inventory of my games box:
- Dice (many different pairs and sizes)
- Pencils (all sharpened)
- Scissors, different sizes and types
- Balls of string, twine, and yarn; clothesline; ribbon
- Tennis, golf, racket, and Ping Pong balls
- A white bed sheet
- Tape (transparent, masking, and duct tape)
- Newspaper and color construction, and scrap paper
- Song books
- Tacks and push pins
- Decks of playing cards

- Feathers
- Beanbags
- Index cards (3 × 5 and 4 × 6)
- Felt-tipped pens and indelible markers
- Rubber erasers
- Crayons, colored chalk
- Alphabet flash cards
- Decorative food picks; toothpicks
- Straight and safety pins and pin cushion
- Lunch bags
- Posterboard and cardboard
- Signs and game templates
- Good quality balloons
- Song titles; list of parables
- Coffee can
- Small trinkets: airplane, model cars, miniature toys; fabric roses, sewing thread, thimble, matchbooks and boxes, buttons, golf tees, navy beans, peanuts, keys
- Socks and pot holder gloves
- Spoons, silver and plastic
- Clothespins
- Paper clips, E-Z clips, and binder clips
- Bells and jingle bells in assorted sizes
- Rubber bike horn (surprise!)
- Party horns
- Decorative tins
- Scarves and blindfolds
- Name tags
- Timer and stopwatch
- Miniature binoculars

To Recap:
Create your own Step-by-Step Planning List.
- Make a Guest List
- Choose a Menu List
- Add a Cleaning List
- Draw a diagram for traffic and serving patterns
- Make up a Games List
- Copy all into your Party Journal Planner
- Start a Games Box

4.
I'M IN THE MOOD FOR . . .

All the really good ideas I ever had came to me while I was milking a cow.
—GRANT WOOD

With the proper atmosphere, you can create winter in the spring, Paris in Peoria, and the fabulous fifties in the 21st century! Mood is more about the scene you set than money. Mood is more important than having the best furnishings or furniture—and it's *less important* than the people in your parade.

Parties take effort, no doubt about it, but don't avoid a party because your chairs don't match, your dining room wall needs painting, or your cooking leaves a lot to be desired. Good friends come to your home because they want to exchange ideas, not measure themselves against you. Remember that Martha Stewart has "good thing" ideas, but she also has the staff and the resources to accomplish them.

Most books about entertaining provide *form over content*—ambitious cuisine on a lovely table in a stunning setting. But put it in perspective: a dozen or more people have pored over the copy, the design, and the photography in order to create those beautiful pictures.

Before you begin, decide what you can handle. Don't let realism be supplanted by fantasy. If you assess your mood and available energy first, you may be able to avoid both the muddling middles (not having enough to do) and the frantic finale (being overwhelmed by having to do too much).

The answers to these problems are simple. Your chairs don't match? Throw slipcovers, sheets, or pillowcases over the offenders and tie them with coordinating bows. Remember though, today's eclectic and aged furniture is *de rigueur*. Dining room wall needs painting? Create a canopy with crepe paper. Fix lovely pastel rolls of crepe paper to the ceiling at the center, tack again at the corner molding, and drape the ends down the walls to form a paper trellis. Add large palms in matching pots and no one will notice your walls. Culinary skills less than dynamic? Throw a soup-making party and have guests bring the ingredients—turn the "Too many cooks spoil the broth" paradigm on its head. Also, make an effort to pick out especially lively games that will keep guests laughing. Good spirits and humor go a long way toward helping you feel fulfilled.

THEME DOS

A large part of mood is theme. And theme is first served by thought—in fact, it's almost a game in itself! There are many good theme-party books on the market and endless ideas for themes. Here are a few of them:

Ice Cream Social
Karaoke
Pizza Night
Sports Theme
Tea Party: Alice in
    Wonderland
Golfer's Birthday
Football Fever
Baby Shower
Groom's Tool Shower
Midnight Prom Buffet
Bridesmaids' Luncheon
Quilter's Block Party
Wine Tasting
Dessert Decadence
Circus Summer
Cookie Exchange for
    Christmas
Stitch 'n' Bitch
Disney Land Party
Computer Club Party
School's Out!
Skill Camp
SOUPer Evening
Bird Count and Party
Mystery Night
Carnival

Recipe Exchange
Scrapbook Fun
Puzzle Night
Book Club or Literary
    Genius Party
Artists' Escape
Dress Up (with Borrowed
    Clothes)
Nifty '50s
Zoo-riffic Birthday Party
Star-Gazer's Gig
Hippie Pad
Anchors Aweigh
Country-Fest
Travel Exchange
Jungle Book
Chinese New Year's
Actors' Workshop/Cast Party
Tailgate Gig
Super Bowl Party
Strawberry Festival
Bike Trip
Painters' Picnic in
    Provence
Around-the-World Party
Life's a Beach
Secret Garden Party

Activities to Combine with Theme Parties

Bread bake
Topiary creations
Egg dyeing and decoration
Pumpkin carving
Cookie frost
Teach me a skill!

Read a play
Paint rocks
Create a silhouette (Victorian
    party)
Make a kite
Collect autographs

Mehendi painting
Crafting
Jewelry making

Flower arranging/wreath
making

But let's see what it would take to make up a theme yourself.

TIME
First, consider the time of the year. A party can be built around a holiday, a season, or a made-up day, such as those created around an event or person. The best examples of these can be found in *Chase's Annual Events*, a guide located in almost all local libraries. Special days, weeks, and months commemorating both the familiar and the strange are listed, such as "National Smile Week," held annually on the first Monday in August through to the following Sunday. How about making up a "Green Eggs and Ham Day" and holding it on Dr. Seuss's date of birth? (Theodore Seuss Geisel was born on March 2, 1904.) Think of the great fun you could have incorporating verse and Seuss characters into your setting. The possibilities are infinite.

INTERESTS

How about building your event around a hobby, avocation, or interest? Several people interested in gardening? You can incorporate flowers and vegetables, tools and implements, and garden-related guessing contests and paper-and-pencil games into the theme. Off the top of my head, I can see creating invitations from seed packets or labels, a game matching botanical names with common names, and serving lemonade from flowered cups and bread or cake baked in clay pots. Some other contests could involve matching glorious photographs to plants, having a "speed plant" or topiary sculpting activity, and blindfolding guests for a fragrant flower smell test. You know, games don't have to be structured to be fun.

A game can be any activity that:
- sets people to thinking; is a test of knowledge or skill
- takes its cue from creativity or making something out of simple objects
- brings people together interactively for a quiz, search, or task
- solves a puzzle or a quiz
- motivates a guest to perform physically or theatrically
- encourages "outgoingness" or a team effort.

SETTING

A theme party in a barn conjures up pictures of fiddles, gingham, and line dancing. Food could be "state fair" cooking, like Grandma Eddy's potato salad, Aunt Betty's first-place blueberry pie, and corn from the field slathered with butter. Guest cowboys and cowgirls could wear dressed-down denim and boots, sit on hay bales, picnic benches, and fence rails. Physically active games would go well in this setting: relays, pitching contests, and even stunts. "People on a String," a tried-and-true popular game from my book *Great Games for Great Parties*, would be at home here and all the more challenging, as people thread a spoon on a string down through their clothes, linking them all together, and then have to pull it back out again.

Safety Tip: Remember to set up a designated smoking area outside the barn, not near the hay, but close to the water trough for safety.

DRESS

As illustrated previously, fancy dress and special attire help to enhance a theme party, and they affect the way people act. A disco ball would call for shiny fabrics, cool suits, and dancing shoes. A variety of "hot potato" or musical games would be great for those who boogie.

Any type of game or matching that brings people together for the first time is certain to be a hit. Dressed for mystery? I once held a mystery party and my guests participated by coming dressed as the 1940s characters they were set to play. Ahead of time I made cardboard dolls of the characters they were to represent and mailed them out with the invitations. They showed up as their alter-egos, wearing name tags sporting their character's name, and dressed in

Steve Watson: Gastonne Schmidt: Yvonne Drake: Major Deegan:

Cybil Admunson: Katie La Femme: Derrick Ellington: Arnold Green:

similar garb to the paper dolls. At intervals throughout the evening a series of clues were given, complete with theme music and audio script. It made for a very creative whodunit and, for the guests, the doll name tags set the mood right from the get-go.

DECORATIONS

Setting the scene with decorations is, personally, my favorite activity when getting ready for a games party. I have used just about everything you can think of to convey a mood or theme, and have yet to exhaust the possibilities. Think about using:

Postcards and posters	Ornaments
Photographs	Colored eggs
Hats and costumes	Children's chairs
Construction paper	Toys
Banners	Stuffed animals, dolls
Big plants	Electronics
Mobiles	Household items
Balloons	Garden tools
Crepe paper	Gift boxes
Confetti	Candles
Flags	Favors
Fabric	Place mats, place cards
Props	Dishware, special serving
Books	pieces
Objects and artifacts	Mirrors
Cutouts and star shapes	Craft items
Collections of related items	Masks
Flowers	Booths
Food; hollowed-out veggies	Tablescapes
Sculpture	Corsages

And the list goes on . . .

INVITATIONS

Invitations are your first big shot at conveying the mood and theme of your party. Think creatively when crafting your invitations. By using small items, decorative paper, and distinctive shapes, you can demonstrate your excitement and communicate a fun approach to entertaining that would make anyone want to come and be part of that mood.

For example, how about using a symbol like a ship for a Bon Voyage party, a box of popcorn for a movie critique group, or a mask for Mardi Gras? Shapes fashioned out of colored construction paper to resemble records, musical notes, pumpkins, love doves—all these things are recognizable and will emphasize your theme.

Here is a list of other things to use for your invitations that you may not have thought of:

Postcards	Nautical flags
Magazine images	Photographs
Theater tickets	Calendar sheet copies
Stamped designs	Play money
Sheet music	Pretend horoscope
Newspaper and pretend ads	Fortune cookies
Small inexpensive flags	Herb labels, soup can labels
Lunch bags	Herb bouquet tied with string
Colored foil	and details attached
Embossed tin	A wooden spoon
Pressed flowers	Playing cards
Lace or paper lace	Bookmarks
Tea bags, packets, seed packets	Games pieces
Confetti	Cartoon characters
Star shapes and foil sticky	Diskette labels
stars	Fake leaves, flowers
Crepe paper	Silhouettes
Colored felt cut into shapes	Party hats, horns
Paper chef's hat	Ribbon (to write on)
Travel brochures	Fabric
Baggage claim tickets	Recipe cards
Report cards, business	Sunday comics
reports, memos	

HERE ARE SOME OTHER IDEAS:

You can make holiday invitation "crackers" by putting theme-related objects in a small mailing tube, wrapping it with crepe paper, and sealing it off by tying the ends with gold cord. Or why not attach some inexpensive charms, coins, or plastic items using curling ribbon, so when the invitation is opened they will dangle out from the bottom?

How about writing the invitation copy on a plastic champagne glass that you hand deliver for a New Year's party? Why not bake a

batch of extra-large sugar cookies in a particular shape and inscribe the details with colored icing pens? Or what about giving away a bubble gum cigar for the birth of your new grandson, attaching the party details to the cigar ring? Learn to fold papers in interesting ways: for example, making the invitation look like a diaper, or using origami to make a Japanese crane, lantern, or other symbol.

You could fashion flannel into a nightcap for a teen sleepover or write on an actual candle for a "Sixteen Candles" birthday celebration. Use the cover of a magazine for a party with a glamour or Hollywood theme. Make a copy of the newspaper on the day the guest of honor was born, reduce it in size on a copying machine, and use the headlines as the cover of your invitation. And don't forget about using different fonts. You might want to write in other styles such as Chinese characters, medieval cursive, or calligraphy to help to convey the mood of a different country, era, or people.

While you are working on invitations, select prizes, favors, and gifts to reflect your theme. That way, when you are out shopping for confetti or construction paper, you may decide to get a prize, gift, or favor along some of the same theme lines, because your brain will be primed for the "Eureka!"—the perfect small gift or item that goes along with your chosen motif. For example, I was invited to give a program to the Hot Springs Village Women's Club. They wanted me to talk about entertaining. I decided to open the agenda with a demonstration game and we played "Barnyard Competition." The day before while shopping, I noticed some plastic chickens set out for Easter. When you pressed on the hen's head, she dispensed a jelly bean into a basket. What a perfect gift to match the game! I couldn't have planned it better.

INVITATION ACCEPTANCE AND FOLLOW-UPS

There is some confusion about when to send invitations, what should be on them, and how to respond. To be honest, there are as many ways to think about invitations and acceptance as there are circumstances. Base your methods on the type of function, your relationship to the guest, how much time you have allotted, and whether or not you need to generate additional interest.

A computer-generated note, an e-mail message, or a phone call will be enough. But your invitation will grow in importance according to:

- the amount of time you've spent on décor and in preparation
- the personal importance this function holds for you
- the amount of driving time and effort involved to get to you.

Another consideration for those of you who are entering into the entertaining game with some amount of trepidation: I have thrown off the shackles of restraint when it comes to follow-up phone calls—many others have, too. I don't feel embarrassed about calling potential guests for responses, and you should not either. It lets you touch base with friends ever so slightly (although this is not the time to catch up on the news with an up-to-the-minute accounting), and gives you the chance to plan intelligently.

JE REGRET NO REGRETS

Most conscientious hosts no longer add the words "regrets only" to a card. Not only does it give an onerous tone to party plans by setting yourself up to listen to the intended guest give excuses or provide some kind of explanation, but it also adds pressure. People's lives are often complicated. The whole point of getting together is to give guests a venue for sharing their goings-on, and to help put friendships and people skills back into perspective. Besides, it really isn't important why people can't come. It may even be embarrassing for them to admit why, so let positive responses be your guide instead.

This next notion might sound amusing, but think about cultivating a relationship with some friend or neighbor who is secure in your friendship and will be happy to fill in for a last-minute canceled guest.

If you have holes at a dinner party you've taken some pains with, call up your mainstay neighbor or reliable old-time friend and ask him/her to join you. They will quick-shower and dress, and be ready to jump in with a smile. An extra cocktail or additional fifteen minutes of chat, and your trustworthy fill-in appears. And maybe this true-blue compadre will bring the unpredictable chemistry and surprise your party needs to maintain a high momentum.

CANCELLATION INSURANCE

Here are some tips about cancellations.

- Inform your guests of the size and nature of the event—for instance, say it will be a sit-down dinner for six, a holiday buffet for twenty-five, or a champagne and dessert reception for a guest of honor plus forty.
- Let them know whether they should eat beforehand.
- Suggest what to wear, or tell them if there is a theme.
- Try to indicate to what extent they would be missed if they were unable to attend.

If, in fact, your guest does phone to cancel, this is where your maturity comes into play, because no one likes to hear about a cancellation. I once read these suggestions—I don't remember where—but they have always helped me (thank you, dear author, whoever you are).

1) Thank your potential guest for calling to tell you, and
2) Assure them that you understand and try to put them at ease without hesitation.
3) Tell them that you will invite them again, and silently examine the predicament from their perspective.
4) Contact your replacement or stand-by friend.
5) Reset the table and change the place card or remove the place setting altogether.
6) Stay calm and let it go; you have other considerations— namely, the guests who are still with you!

MUSIC

Never underestimate the power of music. Music can add drama, atmosphere, and liveliness—or it can overwhelm, overpower, and overstimulate your guests. If you play operatic arias during the dinner part of your games party, you won't encourage conversation. Rap music is too energetic during pencil-and-paper games, and accordion sounds will make young adults giggle. The choice of music and volume needs to be thought out and carefully edited well ahead of time.

It's a good idea to create one long tape or arrange CDs timed to the events of the evening. For example, as guests are arriving maybe some light instrumental jazz will get people circulating and talking. Later, switch to something with dramatic orchestration like synthesizer music to create a competitive aura. While guests are actively playing games, stop the music so as not to interfere with instructions, questions, and natural play. When you break for food, snacks, or dessert, think about picking up the pace a little with, say, flute music for something perky and happy, or saxophone music for a moody or sexy tone. Serve up music as you would different courses of a meal, with each set to stimulate, calm, and satisfy according to good taste.

LIGHTING

Next to comfortable seating, lighting is the single most important factor for a games-party atmosphere. Earlier I asked you to approach your house as a guest would, to get an idea of your home's party curb appeal. I suggest you do the same thing to assess your lighting. Make sure that your guests will not have difficulty coming and going. The main elements to ensure their safety are entry lights and clear pathways. Do whatever you can to "beef up" your outdoor lighting. Use uplights against the house, strong directive lights over walkways and drive, and luminarias to lead the way. When you line the drive with them your house will have a festive glow that says, "This is the place!"

Inside, you have many options. Rheostats installed into otherwise normal lighting allow you to adjust and "dim" the light for party cake presentations or other dramatic events. How will people look under your lights? Pink bulbs usually provide a soft, flattering glow, while amber light throws off a sultry, warm look. You'll need some white light if you expect guests to read instructions, maps, or posters tacked to walls. I have played several newspaper-oriented games, and lighting is the most important factor for competitive players!

Chinese paper lanterns or connected string party lights with low-watt bulbs help to dramatize special food displays. Liquid candles, clear plastic disks filled with wax and wicks, can be floated in bowls with flowers. Fill any object with water topped by a half inch of vegetable oil, and float the disks for a fleet of tiny lights. Uplights will splash a pattern over a wall, or give a plant a special shadow. Picture lights over paintings, bookshelves, and collections will draw people's

eyes in that direction. Just make sure that any especially precious items are either encased or put out of arm's reach at an active games party.

And, finally, I love candles and tapers, but not for a party with activity. I don't want to have to monitor the wax or the flame, taking important time away from the action. If you are set on having them, better delegate the candle responsibility to someone who will check them often. Other than that, votive candles or ones in glass containers or oil lamps are usually safe at the beginning of the evening. If the party lasts longer than four hours though, rely on your volunteer candle assistant once again.

To Recap:
Assess your mood and budget; decide what you can handle.
- Look to calendars, annual events, and made-up festivals to help you choose a theme.
- Use a hobby, vocation, or passionate interest to drive your mood and motif.
- Your setting and mode of dress will dictate your guests' behavior; choose activities accordingly.
- Decorations call for creative brainstorming; don't be afraid to "think out of the box."
- Invitations are your first best shot at drumming up enthusiasm.
- Cultivate a friend who will serve as a party stand-in.
- Communicate your party plans thoroughly.
- Be gracious about cancellations.
- Music is powerful—plan accordingly.
- Lighting enhances mood, and is a must for safety.

5.

THE SIZZLE ON
THE STEAK

The ripest peach is highest on the tree.
—JAMES WHITCOMB RILEY, *THE RIPEST PEACH*

In home decorating, any designer worth his salt will tell you it's a good idea to create at least one "focal point" in a room or setting. An object—*d'art* or not—whether an important fixture of substantial mass and height or a valued labor like *trompe l'oeil*—is something to build a room around. This *focal point* will catch people's attention and draw them in, just as a patron viewing an exhibition might linger over a truly special painting.

With a party or planned event, the focal point will do two things: First, it will restate the theme; and second, it will add an element of surprise, to the delight of your friends.

In order to mastermind such a feat, look for areas where you can offer both theme and surprise. A theme for your table decorations, which I call tablescapes, is a good place to begin. Then, you can look for more ways to incorporate the theme plan into your home. There are many ways to add sizzle.

THE TABLESCAPE

Home décor magazines like *Southern Living, Traditional Home, Southern Accents, Veranda, Martha Stewart's Living,* and *Victoria* often feature ideas for table settings, centerpieces, and table decorations. If I draw a blank when it comes time to think about designing a tablescape, I consult any of these inexpensive guides for a jump start.

Tear the best ideas out of periodicals before you toss them and save them in your party journal. Hole-punch your selections (put regular paper behind the magazine pages so they won't stick in the hole punch) for entry into a 3-ring binder, and paste reinforcements on the holes. Don't worry about duplicating the slick look. The design departments of these magazines spare no expense with table art and, while the designs are upscale showy, they are often rather traditional and short on ingenuity.

One fun element of party planning is to introduce that part of your personality that silently announces, "This is my thing. I love adding my own artful touches to surprise you." At a recent party I attended, the host had some unusual wall art behind the serving table. There were rods on the wall arranged randomly, like pickup sticks; they looked like some kind of exotic tribal weapons or walking sticks. Later, we were all surprised to find out they were just regular dowels painted black, with stripes of bright primary colors painted over the background in ring patterns. Good trick. Here we were so impressed, thinking our host might have been out on safari!

Another time I hosted a regular sorority meeting. Since the members had driven so far to get to my house, I wanted the refreshment portion of the meeting to be something they would remember. I took extra pains to provide some fairly substantial foods like small savory meatballs and cheese sticks for those who would be coming straight from work, and, in addition to the usual fare, an ample relish tray, fruit bites, and a dessert or two. Beverages were a large pot of fresh coffee, cold drinks, and tea.

For the buffet table décor, I started with a quilt in a pleasant tulip pattern. On top of that, I placed a child-sized wooden chair painted in buttermilk blue with country motifs across the back. A small stuffed animal bunny with long ears and carrot-decorated feet was tucked into the arrangement, and I used serving dishes that resembled cabbage leaves and other vegetables. Wild green moss in clay pots for greenery and napkins in floral patterns added to the eclectic mix. None of it was expensive; all the items were collected from around the house, and it made for a nice effect. Since then, I've assembled table designs dozens of times, and it never ceases to be a creative challenge. I look forward to it with each new event.

If you want to use art for the walls or as a personal expression for table décor:

- Think about using regular wood objects like dowels, animal cutouts, or molding purchased from a craft store or home improvement center, painted as accents.
- Place children's doll furniture up on the table for a buffet backdrop. Add stuffed animals or small treasures to complement the setting.
- Don't be afraid to use wild mosses, plain twisted branches, or garden rocks in bowls and pots.
- Add a decorated serving trolley; easy to handle, great for quick cleanups, and another way to restate your theme.

TRENDS

Table decorating trends come and go—matched dishes, gold-leaf charger plates, candles in all shapes and configurations—but the selection and theatricality you add to your table and settings present a chance to reflect your mood, your life, your favorite things.

For a twist on traditional tablescape trends, think about using:

- Baskets, varied bowls, and bottles with textures, shapes, and color.
- Taller items to add height, such as figurines, busts, plaster statues, and wire armatures.
- Large embroidered pieces, or even new clean rag rugs.

And while you're out running errands, don't forget to visit fabric shops or yard goods stores. There are bins filled with:

- Inexpensive cotton prints or discontinued patterns in odd

squares or bolts. Plus, after a holiday, festive-print linen ensembles are really a bargain.

- Metallics or washable, crushed velvets. They make beautiful place mats, and you don't need that much yardage to add a table runner and some wild dash.
- Tapestries and mantel scarves for draping a table.

For an unusual take on table covers, use:

- Movie or art posters.
- Leftover wallpaper or borders.
- Kraft paper or butcher paper with stamped motifs, glue-on sequins, or fake jewels.

Tip: After Christmas look for gold cherubs, small stuffed ornaments that stand up, and sequined or beaded boxes. Along with getting them at 40–70% off, you can stow them away in your closet for use all year round in tablescapes.

Glassware can add a terrific shot of color to any table if you collect it in hues of green, cobalt, amethyst, or red. If you decide to use these pieces, try to keep your dishes neutral or in plain hues and depend on food presentation and the glass colors to enhance the table.

Objects for Tablescapes

- mini topiaries
- pearls
- fans*
- needlework
- decorative teapots
- mini photo frames*
- large pendants
- museum postcards*
- collectible clocks
- elaborate utensils
- silver/gold-wrapped candies
- pyramids of fruit: lemons, etc.
- beautiful pears
- ruffle-leaf cabbages, eggplant
- squashes, avocado
- herb pots*
- Japanese paper unbrellas*
- bottles filled with herbs and oil
- plaster shapes (painted or antique)
- belt buckles
- starfish
- child's blocks*
- dried corn
- découpage ware
- stick candy*
- gargoyles
- tins* and decorative cans
- mini books* and ornate pens
- fabric-wrapped boxes*
- nuts and leaves
- bird's nests and bird houses*
- book stacks

*Starred items can also be used as place cards

- pineapples
- old-style keys
- folk art*
- music boxes
- train cars or model cars
- nautical objects, flags
- Limoges boxes
- garden tools and watering can
- Staffordshire dogs
- rosettes
- tassels, silk cording, gimp
- Murano glass balls
- perfume bottles
- cinnamon sticks
- jars of macaroni or beans
- ceramic tiles*
- small mirrors*
- golden stars or moon cutouts*

- Christmas balls
- studded and scored limes
- grapes
- seed packets
- playing cards*
- golf objects
- sports gear
- 3-dimensional puzzles
- board game pieces
- Easter eggs*
- mini pumpkins*
- clear plastic shapes filled with confetti
- recycled greeting cards*
- marbleized paper
- office supplies*
- mini pillows*
- feathers

*Starred items can also be used as place cards

SURPRISE IDEAS

For the "Surprise!" part of your party, thinking creatively is your best bet. Turn the tables on what is normally expected. For a baby shower, for instance, serve the beverage in baby bottles with straws; wrap the silverware in diapers, and attach diaper pins to the name tags. A funny and simple food game on this basic theme is to have mystery food—jars of baby food set up in number order—and then give the guests paper and pencils, paper plates, and plastic spoons and let them guess the flavor. (Ha! It's not as easy as it sounds! Make sure you peel the defining labels off the jars first.) Children's chairs could be used to serve hors d'oeuvres, hold game supplies, or just act as footstools.

Or, how about forgetting the tablecloth altogether? Spread white butcher paper over the table, supply guests with crayons, and encourage doodling. Cut out the best "artwork" and frame it or laminate it onto cardboard for an inexpensive coaster.

Ever think about serving Oriental take-out in? Put individual portions in take-out containers and have chopsticks for traditionalists, forks and spoons for the others.

At a summer party, you might want to hollow out different types of bread or vegetables to hold condiments, dips, or soup. Your food "shell"—hollowed out apples, tomatoes, and round bread—cuts down on cleanup; sometimes your guests will eat the dish! For a twist, serve soft desserts in small sand pails with tiny shovels as utensils.

Theme-party foods are fairly easy to make—we are most familiar with cakes cut into unique and interesting shapes. In a rush? Don't forget about those fabulous take-out ice cream cakes.

SOUVENIRS, GIFTS, AND GOODIE BAGS

All guests love gifts, and in addition to the ones they can win through the games, if budget allows, think about giving goodie bags. Over the months, check the discount store bins and collect things that relate to your theme idea. If you are having a Round-the-World party, for example, you can find small country flags, pencils with international themes, maps, travel-size toothbrushes, compasses, paper umbrellas, Perugina chocolates, and fortune cookies. Put vintage-looking stickers on the bags or dangle a fake lei around the handles. (Maybe you could even make up your own "Passport" invitations. See? Theme thinking is contagious!)

SOME OTHER NICE IDEAS

Why not think about tying the invitations to a prize, or creating a lottery ticket from colored paper that can be redeemed at the party?

Don't forget how dramatic lighting can be. Test different hues of bulbs—pink, soft white, and natural light. Use uplights or clips-ons for wall art, perhaps highlighting some branches you've sprayed with white, gold, or silver paint. Likewise, a roaring fire makes a warming light flicker and casts a glow of well-being. A safety note: Have adequate tools and fire screens to fence the area off. A designated "fire chief" should keep an eye on it.

Wrought-iron garden chairs can bring spring to a corner. Sprigs of freesia, a fragrant gardenia, or a rose pinned onto a ribbon will add a festive summer surprise for the guests' hair or lapel no matter what the season.

Talented friends? Make arrangements ahead of time for a little piano music or a magic trick or two—nice for a change of pace while guests are eating. Just don't let it turn into a recital or a stage show—five to ten minutes is tops.

Tip: Since you have gone the extra mile to make sure your party has "Sizzle," why don't you also have a designated photographer? That way, you and your guests will be able to "Remember the time . . ." Order lots of sets for giveaway, or e-mail pictures taken with your digital camera.

To Recap:
- Think about focal points: something to draw your guests in.
- Tablescapes are easy to create; save magazine clippings and ideas in your party journal.
- Don't be afraid to use household objects or collectibles for tablescapes.
- Experiment with different types of tablecloths for texture and interest.
- Look for crossover theme ideas that help to coordinate your table, your décor, and your games.
- Brainstorm your theme idea to create Surprise! gift and goodie bags.
- Consider getting a designated photographer to film the event.

6.
PRE-PARTY GAMES, CONTESTS, AND ICEBREAKERS

We must always change, renew, rejuvenate ourselves; otherwise we harden.
— JOHANN WOLFGANG VON GOETHE

PRE-PARTY GAMES

Pre-party games accomplish several purposes. Most important, these activities help to establish the tone and mood for the rest of the party. Pre-party action is usually needed while waiting for a larger group to assemble. It gives early arrivals something to do other

than sit and wait, and it helps to keep them from feeling lost in a large room before others get there. Also, for people who are not acquainted, the pre-party contest creates a feeling of belonging. A quiz, hunt, or shared project is a good way for people to become acquainted. And finally, the best reason for inducing your company into "self action" is that you will be free to act as greeter, a position that, personally, I am very reluctant to give up.

Name of the game: D.I.Y.

Type: Pre-party defroster.   **# of players:** Any

Supplies: Table with all sorts of materials and scraps: construction paper, fabric, aluminum foil, cellophane, pipe cleaners, crepe paper, ribbon, felt, decorative material. *Tools:* scissors, sticky tape, stick glue, regular white glue, crayons, pencils, ruler, pins, and staple gun.

Formation: Casual seating in readily available chairs, or standing.

Object of the game: For guests to create something as they arrive. It may be a hat or part of a costume; perhaps they will help with a name tag, place mat, or place card, or maybe even an unfinished decoration. You can incorporate the "creation" into the program later, or give it to a favorite hospital or charity.

Play action: Have a few finished samples and some available patterns on hand for those who do not feel very creative. It is fun for two people to work together and you may want to encourage that. Allow 15 or 20 minutes.

Hints and tips: Decorate a hat; make Christmas decorations; help with a centerpiece; make a decorated egg, mask, or a little scene.

Name of the game: Map of Treasure Island

Type: Pre-party contest.   **# of players:** Any

Supplies: Draw a large map of an imaginary island with as many different features as possible. Divide the map into small squares by inking in horizontal lines from top to bottom (number those lines) and vertical lines from left to right (give those lines letters). Make or buy small flags with pins attached (one for each guest), and write a guest's name on each one.

Formation: Casual mingling.

Object of the game: To stake your claim.

Play action: Decide upon the place where the treasure is hidden—choose an intersection, such as C5 or G7. Decide on a few other places for "traps" and note these intersections, too. Affix the map to a board—foam board is great for this—and place it in a prominent position. As guests arrive, invite them to stake their claim to the treasure by sticking their flag on any intersection of lines. Later in the evening, after a break for refreshments, declare the winner (the flag nearest the treasure spot) and give a prize. The unfortunates who stuck their flag on a trap, however, must pay a forfeit. (See pages 114-121.)

Adaptation: Pressed for time? Use any map that has the grid pattern.

Name of the game: Ringing the Bottle

Type: Pre-party contest (old carnival game).

# of players: Small group or individual play

Supplies: Long-necked bottle; curtain ring on a string, tied to a pole, dowel, or cane; chalk or masking tape to make a line; prizes for winners.

Formation: Individual stands in a marked circle or behind a line.

Object of the game: To get the ring over the neck of the bottle, three times.

Play action: Place a bottle on the floor and let players try to ring the bottle.

Hints and tips: Try to ring the bottle yourself before you set it out for use. You may have to adjust the bottle size or curtain ring size to make it possible. Have several different areas so that more than one can play at the same time. To make it more difficult, have players set a time clock for each try, say three minutes. Set the time to coordinate with difficulty.

Name of the game: Statue of Love

Type: Skit/defroster.   **# of players:** Small group

Supplies: Chair; a male accomplice; a half orange; a blindfold; a victim.

Formation: The victim is blindfolded and told that she " . . . will be privy to historical art at its finest!" The accomplice stands on a chair, stiff like a statue.

Object of the game: Fun play and to warm up a crowd.

Play action: The leader, in his/her best oratorical style, says something like: "This is an incredible journey into the world of culture and art. I want you to feel the art with me. In front of you is a statue of the great Lord Byrus, a man of strength and poise. Feel the strength in the Lord's powerful legs." (Run the victim's hand up and down the statue's calves.) "Be aware of the strength in his sinewy arms." (The victim feels arms, pectorals, etc.) "This is the mouth that melted the kisses of Lady-So-Eager, and this is the nose that smelled the coming of the brutal enemy, the tribe known as the Want-Its." At this point, the leader passes one half of an orange to his accomplice, the statue, and, the leader thrusts the victim's fingers into the pulpy middle of the orange while saying, "And this is his EYE!"

Name of the game: Quick Switch

Type: Icebreaker or shower game.   **# of players:** Small group

Supplies: Chairs in a circle; prize is optional.

Formation: Players are seated, one stands in middle.

Object of the game: To warm everyone up.

Play action: The player in the middle calls out something like, "All those wearing wristwatches change places." As they change, the person in the middle tries to secure a seat, and the one player left without a chair continues in the middle.

Hints and tips: The guest of honor (if there is one) should be the first person in the middle. Decide on at least seven changes to give different players a chance to be the person in the middle. You can give a booby prize to anyone who winds up in the middle three times.

Phrases to name:
All those wearing tennis shoes.
All those wearing glasses.
All those with blue eyes.
All those wearing white, and so on.

Name of the game: Listen

Type: Pre-party self-play.   **# of players:** Small group

Supplies: Eight matchboxes numbered and filled with: 1) straight pins; 2) navy beans or dried peas; 3) rice; 4) matches; 5) BBs; 6) paper clips; 7) tacks; 8) sand (you can add others: candy corn; screws, etc.); pencil and papers for answers.

Formation: Informal gathering and mingling.

Object of the game: Guess what is in each box.

Play action: Shaking boxes and making guesses. Later, collect papers and score. The most correct answers wins a prize.

Hints and tips: Try it yourself ahead of time and add or vary ingredients as you see fit. You can also award a prize for the "most creative" answer.

Name of the game: Smell Test

Type: Pre-party contest.   **# of players:** Small group

Supplies: Baking tins (foil cupcake papers will do) each with a cotton ball, dabbed with a liquid and numbered; pencil and paper for players; prizes.

Formation: Cups set on table, players mingle.

Object of the game: To guess the smell. The most correct answers wins a prize.

Play action: Competitors may touch the cups but not the cotton.

Hints and tips: Vanilla is easy. Hide a coffee bean, peppercorns, vinegar, a garlic clove, mustard seeds, a peppermint, almond and orange extract; there are a lot of choices for smells. (Seeds and cloves can be crushed and hidden in the cotton.)

Adaptation #1: Cups filled with spices. No tasting!

Adaptation #2: Cups filled with cubes of cheese. For this game version, you can have a cube of cheese for each player to taste test, if you prefer. Mini foil cups are great—only one cube per player, please!

Adaptation #3: Can be played as an individual or team contest— blindfold the competitors.

Name of the game: Guessing

Type: Pre-party self-contest.   **# of players:** Any number

Supplies: Paper and pencil; guessing accoutrements; prizes for closest correct answers.

(*No touch* examples):

Jar of peanuts	How many?
Orange with seeds	Number of seeds?
Scrap of newspaper	Number of printed words?
Glass of water	Quantity (in ounces)?
Dictionary	Number of pages?
Table lamp	Height?
Long string	Length?
Photo of baby	Age?
Stack of notes	Number of sheets?
Head of lettuce	Weight?

Formation: Use one or more of these items set out on a table. Number each item you use and indicate whether you need the weight, number of pages, and so on.

Object of the game: To come closest to the correct answer.

Play action: Guests may not pick up or touch objects in any way.

Hints and tips: This activity can be done without verbal directions or monitoring. Construct a stand-up sign with the instructions printed on it; advise players to leave signed answer sheets in a box. Hold the contest open until, say, 9:00 p.m. Sometime after 9 p.m., your assistant can check the guesses against the correct amounts. Give one small prize for each closest guess.

Name of the game: Building Matches

Type: Pre-party table game.   **# of players:** 5/6 to a group

Supplies: For each group, a soda bottle and box of wooden matches; prizes.

Formation: Players sit around a table, each with a handful of matches.

Object of the game: To place your match successfully.

Play action: Players, in turn, place a matchstick on top of the open bottle so that it will balance there. The object is to see how many they can pile up on the bottle.

Hints and tips: Play is competitive between teams. The biggest stack wins.

Name of the game: Postage-Stamp Find

Type: Pre-party icebreaker.   **# of players:** Any

Supplies: Several postage stamps and willing guests; 3 prizes.

Formation: Guests mingle until three winners come forward.

Object of the game: To find the two postage-stamp wearers (or more, depending on size of party—for example, 2 stamp wearers for 20 guests, 3 for 30, and so on).

Play action: As guests arrive, you meet and greet. Pick out two individuals—not necessarily a couple—to wear a postage stamp (the stamps do not have to be identical). When all arrive, announce the object of the game and begin to play. When a guest has spotted the two stamps, he or she comes to the host and quietly tells who is wearing them. The first three people to identify the stamp-wearers win a prize.

Hints and tips: Try to obscure the stamp by placing it against something of the same color or in a busy pattern.

ICEBREAKER GAMES

These games are also referred to as "defrosters" or "chill chasers," and are sometimes thought to be the same as "get-acquainted" games. A subtle distinction exists between the two: Get-acquainted games are primarily designed to help people learn and practice the names of the other guests. Introductions are emphasized and names are pronounced slowly and loudly. You, as leader, repeat the person's name no matter who announces it, because people have a tendency to hurry or speak softly when in the spotlight.

Icebreakers encourage intermingling and conviviality. They stimulate conversation and create a relaxed atmosphere by causing people to think, work, and interact with one another. For both sets of games, though, the leader needs to understand the directions implicitly, so as not to confuse people when explaining them. The major effort should go into the action rather than finding out what to do. Also, don't let any activity drag on too long or become too familiar.

One other note: These activities can be used at any point in the games program. Try interspersing them with relays or stunts for a change of pace.

Name of the game: One-Word Conversation

Type: Get-acquainted.   **# of players:** Any

Supplies: None.

Formation: Any size group, large or small, scattered about the floor in pairs; pairs are numbered 1 and 2.

Object of the game: To meet and greet.

Play action: On a signal, the number 1s carry on a conversation with their number 2s using only ONE word at a time. They are to find out as much as possible about that person. On a second signal, number 2s ask number 1s the questions. When "Change" is called, everyone turns, finds another partner, and the questioning begins again.

Hints and tips: Sample:

Name? Jane Johnson	Business? Architecture
Home? San Diego	Hobby? Stained glass
Married? No	Sport? Skiing
Children? No	College? Yale

Adaptations: This game can be played quite easily with the person on either side of a guest at a banquet or dinner party. Don't let too much time pass for each encounter.

Name of the game: Tissue Tournament

Type: Team icebreaker.   **# of players:** Any, teams

Supplies: For each player—drinking straws; pieces of tissue; prizes for winning team.

Formation: Players standing in line.

Object of the Game: To finish first.

Play action: Each player holds a straw in his or her mouth. The leader of each team places a piece of tissue paper over the end of the straw and breathes in, causing the paper to be held in place at the end of the straw. The leader must then pass the tissue to the next player, who passes it on, until the first team finished wins.

Hints and tips: The secret of a successful pass is that the first player must breathe out gently as the second player breathes in. The paper must not be touched by hand, but if it falls to the ground, the player who dropped it is allowed to pick it up by hand and return it to its position at the end of the straw.

Name of the game: Memory Game

Type: Get-acquainted.   **# of players:** Any

Supplies: None.

Formation: Players seated in a circle.

Object of the game: To help everyone learn and remember names.

Play action: This is one of a variety of word games based on the participants' remembering things or the order of things in a list, such as the children's "I'm going to Africa and I'm going to take_____." Of course, the blank is filled with whatever comes into the player's mind, and then this phrase is repeated, going around the circle, adding phrases in order until someone misses. In this version the leader starts. For example, I would say, "*I am Andy, Antsy Andy.*" This phrase is picked up by my neighbor who says, "*That is Antsy Andy, I am Zany Zelda.*" So the phrases are repeated. Each time the players add on their own name and an adjective describing themselves with the same letter as their first name.

Hints and tips: It's no surprise that later, during the course of the event, a guest will be referred to by his/her newly coined name—Bashful Betsy or Terrible Terry!

Name of the game: Something Odd

Type: Icebreaker.   **# of players:** Large mixer

Supplies: Six willing conspirators will have something odd about the way they dress (confer ahead of time); pencil and paper for all.

Formation: Mixing in.

Object of the game: To be the first person to find the correct six.

Play action: The six odd guests circulate, and the first guest to discover what is "odd" writes it down along with the name of the guest.

Ideas for oddities:

Missing earring	Odd-colored socks
A pin upside down or	Watch worn upside down
on the back of a suit or dress	Mismatched shoes
Necktie in a bow	

And so on . . . the possibilities may be quite funny.

Name of the game: Balloon Anklets

Type: Active/get-acquainted.　　**# of players:** Couples or pairs

Supplies: Balloons, string.

Formation: Casual standing. Balloons are blown up quite large and tied around the ankle of each player, toward the back.

Object of the game: To stomp and break the competitor's balloons.

Play action: On a signal, players try to break the others' balloons but keep their own intact.

Adaptations: Balloons can be tied at waist height, pulled around to the back, and swatted with rolled-up newspapers.

Name of the game: Couples Quiz

Type: Icebreaker/　　**# of players:** Small group,
　　get-acquainted.　　　　　　　　divided into couples

Supplies: Planned questions; pencil and paper.

Formation: Couples.

Object of the game: To get the most points.

Play action: One half of each couple leaves the room. The others remain and are asked questions about their partner, spouse, or date. They answer the question the way they think their partner would respond. The answers are written down. The missing partners return, are each asked the same questions, and give their own answers. One point is logged for each match. Then, the other half of each couple leaves, new questions are asked, and the roles are reversed.

Name of the game: Calling Card

Type: Get-acquainted for strangers.   **# of players:** Any

Supplies: Business card from each guest (arrange ahead of time); hat or basket to pick from.

Formation: Guests circulate.

Object of the game: Introductions and for meeting new people.

Play action: Guests pick one business card and try to match it with the owner. After ten minutes, everyone reveals their profession. Allow them to tell stories about their "intuitive" feelings.

Name of the game: Dollar Shakedown

Type: Defroster and   **# of players:** Any, fairly
     get-acquainted.   large group

Supplies: Silver dollars, helpers.

Formation: Circulating guests.

Object of the game: To earn some cash and meet some people.

Play action: A few confederates receive three silver dollars each. Choose one confederate for every five to ten guests. The host then announces that a few people in the room are holding money and a coin will be given to the lucky fifth, tenth, and fifteenth guest to shake their hand. Everyone will shake hands all around.

Hints and tips: Confederates must keep silent count and act as sly as possible. The money spent is worth it.

Name of the game: Rogue's Gallery

Type: Defroster and get-acquainted.   **# of players:** Any

Supplies: Full sheets of large-size—minimum 11" × 14" (28 × 35 cm)—drawing paper, sticky tack, lamp; crayon, chalk, or pastel stick; pencil and paper for guessing.

Formation: As guests arrive, stand (or sit) them near the silhouette wall. Take the shade off the lamp with the light source in front of the subject; it will cast a wonderful shadow. Position the paper over the shadow, stick it to the wall, and experiment to find the best distance at which to stand. Using your crayon, chalk, or pastel stick, trace the line of the shadow to create a silhouette. This is very easy, no artistic skill required. Lightly pencil in a number at the bottom. (Do not let anyone see the results.)

Object of the game: Fun identification.

Play action: Sometime later in the evening, hang the portraits on the wall and let your guests see how many they recognize, matching the silhouette to its owner.

Name of the game: Who Am I Tonight?
Type: Defroster and get-acquainted   **# of players:** Large group
Supplies: Name cards, string- or ribbon-bound for a necklace.
Formation: Guests mixing.
Object of the game: To guess your identity.
Play action: This game is an alternate version of one of the best defroster games ever, "Who Am I?" It is great for introducing new players. As each guest arrives, he or she receives a name card, which is hung down the back. Men get a card with the name of a woman who is present. Women get one with the name of a man who is present. Guests are turned loose to ask questions that can only be answered with a "yes" or "no." No other questions are legal. Say, for example, he asks, "Am I a blonde?" If the answer is "Yes," he looks around and discovers four blondes present. When he thinks he knows who he is, he approaches his choice and asks, "Am I Ruth Murray?" If he is she, he may remove his card.

Name of the game: Who Is This?
Type: Defroster.   **# of players:** Any
Supplies: Cut photographs of well-known people from newspapers or magazines. Paste the images on poster board, number them, and hang them up; pencil and paper for players.
Formation: Guests mix.
Object of the game: To get the most correct answers.
Play action: Players guess the names of the people pictured, write down their answers.
Hints and tips: Use several boards and space them out, because

people will congregate. You can increase or decrease the difficulty of this game by the photos chosen.

Adaptation: Choose photos of sports figures for an athletic group, politicians for a business meeting, performers for a mixed group, etc.

Name of the game: Matchbox Cram

Type: Defroster.   **# of players:** Any, couples

Supplies: Matchbox for each pair playing; timer or signal; prizes.

Formation: Players hunt all over the house (and yard, if designated).

Object of the game: To fill the matchbox with the most items.

Play action: Players are dispatched to collect tiny items, such as paper clips, safety pins, rice kernels, dried beans, peppercorns, ribbon, tacks, and so on. No article may be used more than once. When "time" is called, the items are counted and the prize is awarded.

Hints and tips: You may want to declare certain areas off limits. And you may have to set up a penalty for torn boxes, etc.

Name of the game: Costume Party

Type: Defroster.   **# of players:** Any

Supplies: Guests bring three items of old clothing (for male or female); prizes (optional).

Formation: Guests mingling.

Object of the game: Creative costuming.

Play action: Each guest takes items from the "collection," and creates unique outfits. An impromptu modeling show takes place.

Hints and tips: Take pictures and give "booby" prizes for the best feminine look, best seasonal attire, and so on.

Name of the game: Object Hunt

Type: Defroster.   **# of players:** Large group up to 50

Supplies: Prize for winner: a large bar of chocolate.

Formation: Guests mingle.

Object of the game: To find objects 1 through 6 "conscientiously" from object to object (honor system), not skipping any, but to be the first one done.

Play action: Arrangements are made with six people privately, before the party begins. They are each to represent a different object—let's say 1) a sponge, 2) a capuchin monkey, 3) a pumpkin pie, 4) a juvenile judge, 5) a Belgian waffle, and 6) a bar of chocolate. You explain the game and their respective roles. The rest of the guests have to find out who or what these six people are, working their way from one to the other, until #6 has been reached. Six has the prize—the bar of chocolate. The players are told the first thing they have to find is a sponge, and that the sponge will tell them what to look for next. So, to begin, everyone says to everyone else, "Are you a sponge?" When the sponge is found by a player, he whispers, "Right, now look for a capuchin monkey." The monkey, when found, whispers, "Yes, now look for a pumpkin pie." And so on.

Hints and tips: The six confederates should act as if they are players.

Name of the game: Jigsaw Puzzle

Type: Defroster.   **# of players:** Large group

Supplies: Picture postcards, one for every four players. On the plain side of each card, write the name of an animal eight times. Then cut the cards into eight pieces, each with one word on it. There will be eight "tigers," eight "elephants," and so on.

Formation: Guests mix; prepare for a great scramble.

Object of the game: The players are to find all eight pieces and re-form the postcards.

Play action: The postcard pieces are jumbled and scattered around the room. Tell each four players to collect all pieces marked "tiger"; and so on. When they find their eight pieces, they proceed to a table to fit them together. First postcard completed wins a prize.

Hints and tips: The cards can be cut into smaller pieces to make the game more difficult. Use different postcard pictures for added variety.

Name of the game: Portrait Gallery

Type: Defroster and get-acquainted.   **# of players:** Any

Supplies: Everyone supplies a photo of him/herself as a child or baby; pencil and paper.

Formation: Gallery-type viewing.

Object of the game: Identifying the pictures. Winner has most correct.

Play action: Viewers write on their paper the number and name of the person identified.

Hints and tips: Photos may be passed around one at a time, if preferred. Use post-it notes to number the photos, either on the wall or on the back so as not to damage precious pictures.

Adaptation: If the participants already know the photos, have them guess the age of the participant when the photo was taken.

7.
QUIET GAMES AND TABLE GAMES

Never eat at a place called Mom's. Never play cards with a man named Doc. And never lie down with a woman who's got more troubles than you.—NELSON ALGREN, *WHAT EVERY YOUNG MAN SHOULD KNOW*

"**Q**uiet" games are inactive games (not necessarily quiet verbally.) They include pencil-and-paper, word problems, guessing, and memory games. They are wonderful for changing the pace of a party and stimulating your guests' thinking skills. The mental competition involved may require a quick response, and the questions or puzzles can be as hard as your group is intelligent. Always aim high—you will be surprised at how much everyone knows. In table games people are seated around a table or need to make use of a table. Many of them are pencil-and-paper games.

If you have quick access to a copying machine, prepare your papers ahead of the party. It saves time explaining and things usually run faster. (Hang onto your master copy and put it in your games box for future parties.)

If you will be dictating a list of items or instructions for a task, move slower when people are writing and repeat the information at least once.

Prepare name tags and use them in the games. Tags can be worn or turned over for facts, directions, or a surprise. (Hiding information underneath cups or chair seats is another fun way to transmit instructions or give away prizes or gifts.)

For ease in scorekeeping, hand the participants a playing card, a coin, or a piece of candy for them to collect as they win rounds or points. Don't be surprised if they eat their points!

Name of the game: Area Quiz
Type: Pencil-and-paper.   **# of players:** Small group
Supplies: Prepared questions; paper and pencils.
Formation: Seated.

Object of the game: To get the most correct answers. (May exchange papers to score.)

Play action: True and false questions about area and state. (Can use: state flower, state flag, tree, symbol, etc.)

Hints and tips: Throw in funny questions like: The area's festival queen is called "Miss Bathhouse." "The police K-9 is a Rottweiler." Look for little-known oddities or trivia about your area for added fun.

Adaptation: Use politics too—for example, the state representative, senator, and so on.

Name of the game: Five Square

Type: Pencil-and-paper.   **# of players:** Any

Supplies: Copies of a template that resembles a blank crossword drawn on paper. It consists of twenty-five squares, five each way. Each should be large enough to hold a clearly written letter; pencils.

Formation: Seated comfortably with a surface to write on.

Object of the game: To make as many complete words as possible, the longer the better.

Play action: Play begins by one person calling out any letter he or she likes. The players must then write this letter in any square they choose on their paper. The second player calls out a letter and the action is repeated until all squares are filled. Words are counted when they are spelled from left to right across, down, or on the two diagonals from the top corners. Scoring: 5-letter words get five points; four-letter words 4 points; and so on. There can be more than one word in a line—every word is counted. Add up points until a winner is found.

Name of the game: The Good Ole Days

Type: Pencil-and-paper.   **# of players:** Any
  Use for "honored" guest or birthday.

Supplies: Do some research ahead of time, about the year the guest of honor was born. Develop questions around the newsworthy events or facts of that year; pencil and paper.

Formation: Casual seating.

Object of the game: To get the most correct answers.

Play action: After you've distributed pencil and paper, pose the "good ole days" questions.

Examples of questions:
- What were the popular songs? TV shows? Radio programs?
- What movie won the Academy Award?
- What was the price of bread? Milk? Coffee? Car?
- What was invented that year?
- Who was president?
- Name a fad.

Sometimes the answers will be very entertaining. Read some aloud.

Name of the game: Personal Favorites

This is best played by a small group of friends
who meet regularly or know each other well . . .

Type: Pencil-and-paper.   **# of players:** Small group

Supplies: Pencils and paper.

Formation: Casual seating.

Object of the game: Get to know each other better.

Play action: The leader asks everyone to write down "six things you could never have too much of." When all are finished, they sign their papers and hand them in. The leader reads them while everyone tries to guess whose list is being read. Writers must confess if no one guesses.

Hints and tips: Ask for some minor elaboration, if interesting.

Name of the game: Set the Table

Type: Pencil-and-paper.   **# of players:** Any

Supplies: Paper and pencils.

Formation: Casual seating.

Object of the game: Most correct answers.

Play action: Read questions aloud. All answers end with TABLE.

Questions: **Answers:**
1) A table you cannot copy.   Inimitable
2) A table for the meatless.   Vegetable
3) very delightful table.   Delectable
4) A table easily annoyed.   Irritable

5) A table to suit any purpose.	Adaptable
6) A table you can sell.	Marketable
7) A table to relax on.	Comfortable
8) A table that earns its keep.	Profitable
9) A table that is not right.	Unsuitable
10) A table easy to carry.	Portable
11) A table that will not be left behind.	Unforgettable
12) A table you cannot question.	Indubitable
13) A table you cannot avoid.	Inevitable
14) A table not fit to be seen.	Disreputable
15) A table that is pleasant to the taste.	Palatable
16) A table worthy of esteem.	Respectable
17) A table you cannot improve.	Unbeatable
18) A table of importance.	Notable
19) A table worth repeating.	Quotable
20) A table that is boundless.	Illimitable

Name of the game: Consequences
This is the original game of Consequences.

Type: Pencil-and-paper.   **# of players:** Small group

Supplies: A large index card with instructions written on it, to be passed around; extra paper, extra pencils.

Formation: Players seated in a circle.

Object of the game: To create a very funny story.

Play action: Each player receives the instruction card one at a time along with the paper and a pencil. The first person writes down the first item at the top of the paper, turns down the edge so that his/her response is hidden, and hands the instruction card and the paper and pencil to the next person, who writes down the second item just below the folded edge, and turns down the paper again. At the end, all items are read by the leader, with connecting words used for continuity.

Hints and tips: This game is very old and very traditional. It works best with guests who know each other well. Some preparation is needed to make up the instruction card.

The Instruction Card
1) Write two adjectives describing a man.
2) Write a man's name.
3) Write two adjectives describing a woman.

4) Write a woman's name.
5) Write down a place.
6) Write down an object.
7) Write something a man says to a woman.
8) Write something a woman says to a man.
9) Write down a set of consequences, e.g., go to the beach; run for president; embarrassed his mother; went bankrupt, etc.
10) Write down a comment of: What the world said.

Here is the story outline, which the leader reads aloud while inserting the answers:

The ___(1) and ___(1) *(descriptive adjectives)* ___(2) *(man's name)* met the___(3) and ___(3) *(adjectives)* ___(4) *(woman's name)* at the ___(5) *(where they met)*. He gave her___(6) *(object)* and he said, "___"(7) *(what a man says)*. She said to him, "___"(8) *(what a woman says)*. The consequence was___(9) *(a consequence)*. And the world said, "___" (10) *(what the world said)*.

Name of the game: Birthday
This an adaptation of Consequences.

Type: Pencil-and-paper.   **# of players:** Small group

Follow the same instructions as for Consequences.
1) Today's date.
2) Two adjectives describing a person.
3) Birthday boy or girl's name.
4) Two or more adjectives.
5) Name of a good friend.
6) What I wanted for my birthday.
7) What I got.
8) What it cost, amount of money.
9) Where it was bought, a discount store, an office supply, etc.
10) Who gave it to me.
11) What I did with it.
12) What everyone said about it.

When you read the story, alter it to fit the circumstances. For example: On the ___ (1) *(date)*, ___ (2) *(adjective)* ___ (3) *(birthday name)* asked ___ (4) *(two adjectives)* (5. *name of friend)* to get him a birthday gift. He wanted ___ (6) *(name of desired item)* and he got ___ (7) *(what he got)*. It cost ___ (8) *(an amount of money)*. It was purchased at ___ (9) *(where it was purchased)*. After some questions he found out that ___ (10) *(who gave it)* really picked it out, and he ___ (11) *(what he did with it)*. Everyone was shocked and said ___ (12*) (what they said)*!

Name of the game: Last Night   **# of players:** Small group
This is another version of Consequences.

The questions are as follows—shorter story. Create scenario to match.
1) Where did you go last night?
2) What did you do there?
3) Who did you see there?
4) What did they say?
5) What did you say?
6) Then what happened?
7) How did the evening end?

Name of the game: What Do You Know?

Type: Pencil-and-paper
    team competition.

# of players: Teams of
    4 or more

Supplies: Prepared questions or puzzles—devise your own and make copies for each team; pencils; team prize.

Formation: Small groups seated together with a captain for each team.

Object of the game: To be all-around geniuses or the top "Mensa group" or whatever title strikes you as best.

Play action: Leader (you) sits apart from the teams and hands each captain of a team a puzzle for the team to work on. Upon completion, it is checked, and, if correct, the team is given another to solve.

Ideas for puzzles:
• An unpunctuated sentence or paragraph
• The outlines of various road signs (or international signs)—teams must fill in their meanings
• Names of books—needing authors' names
• Scrambled words or phrases
• Run-on proverbs without vowels
• A math problem (for the engineers in the group)

Name of the game: The Estimators

Type: Pencil-and-paper.   **# of players:** Any

Supplies: Take specific measurements of the room beforehand. Have numbers on hand; pencils and paper.

Formation: Guests seated.

Object of the game: To come closest to the correct answer.

Play action: Guests try their skill at estimating.
1) Height of room
2) Length of room
3) Area of window space
4) Width of window
5) Height of fireplace
6) Diameter of table
7) Total width of curtains, etc.

Name of the game: Word Association

Type: Pencil-and-paper/   **# of players:** Any, small
    psychological game.   group of friends

Supplies: Decide on one or two
    common words; stopwatch if desired.

Formation: Casual seating.

Object of the game: Insight into others.

Play action: Word associations do give insight into what you are thinking. Tell your guests you are going to give them one word and they must immediately write down on their paper the first 15 words that pop into their heads. They must play fair and you can limit their time to ensure that. If you say "temple" and count to 20 while they are writing, they won't have much chance to fake. After they have all written the first 15 words that pop into their heads, have them write their names on the paper and exchange it with their neighbor. Each list is read aloud and it is up to the guests to "analyze" the author.

Name of the game: Say It with Two

Type: Pencil-and-paper.   **# of players:** Any

Supplies: List of definitions; prize.

Formation: Casual seating.

Object of the game: Answers for all the definitions.

Play action: Read the list. Players write down phrases. Give examples:

Phrase	Answer
not difficult	E-Z
number that follows 79	A-T

Then, players are to find the two letters that match the definition.

1)	devoid, barren	M-T
2)	disintegrate	D-K
3)	a girl's name	K-T
4)	of whatever quantity	N-E
5)	prior to	B-4
6)	a fabric	P-K
7)	an electric unit	O-M
8)	to lead in a particular field	X-L
9)	milestone age	4-D
10)	with flair	R-T
11)	a greeting	L-O
12)	sly, clever	K-G
13)	Indian home	T-P
14)	an attorney	D-A
15)	beer or stout	A-L

Phrase	Answer
16) dog	K-9
17) award for TV	M-E
18) leafy vegetable	K-L
19) type of pasta	Z-T
20) famous batter	K-C
21) music minder	D-J
22) to skin	P-L
23) a girl's name	L-N

Name of the game: Whose Nose?

Type: Pencil-and-paper, guessing.

# of players: Small group, no more than 20

Supplies: Old bedsheet, non-marking masking tape; scissors; numbered sign-up sheet; pencils and paper.

Formation: Split the group in half: for example, 10 and 10—some players behind the sheet, the rest guessing.

Object of the game: To figure out whose nose is whose.

Play action: Stretch a sheet across an open door. It has a small hole in it a little less than eye height. The players behind the sheet take turns pressing their noses through the hole. You keep track of them in number order. The onlookers, trying to guess whose nose it is, will number and write down their guesses.

NOSE

Hint and tips: Sound easy? It's not! Hilarious. Some couples do not even recognize each other's noses.

Name of the game: Sherlock on the Town

Type: Pencil-and-paper.   **# of players:** Any

Supplies: A list of mystery phrases that describe well-known restaurants and areas of interest in your town. Pick 18–20 of your favorite places. Type or print the list and make copies, one for each player.

Formation: Casual seating.

Object of the game: Best " detective" wins a prize.

Play action: Players solve riddle clues. For example:

Lots of cents	J.C. Penny's
To singe	Sears
Had a farm	McDonald's
Strong angle of wall	Cornerstone Plaza
Acorn-grass area	Oaklawn Racetrack

Hints and tips: This is a great activity for a "newcomer's party."

Name of the game: Creating Ghosts

Type: Creative thinking.   **# of players:** Small group

Supplies: Hershey kisses (3 for each player).

Formation: Casual circle.

Object of the game: Not to become a ghost.

Play action: Start a player off with a common pair of words, such as "lunch box." The next player must attach another common pair of words to this pair and so on until someone gets stuck and can't go on. Anyone who can't continue, eats a kiss (or turns it in) and starts a new pair. The first player to lose all three kisses is a ghost and no one can speak to him/her for the rest of the game.

Example: On the starting pair of words "lunch box"
    2nd player: box spring
    3rd player: spring time
    4th player: time lock
    5th player: lock up. . .
    10th player: I can't continue. My new pair is "full house."

Adaptation: Use a stopwatch for shorter response times.

Name of the game: One Minute to Go

Type: Thinking game.   **# of players:** Small group

Supplies: Watch or timer; pencil and paper; assistant.

Formation: Casual seating.

Object of the game: Player with the most words wins.

Play action: You—the leader—tell your guests that you will name a letter (not X). After you name the letter, the person on your right must name as many words as he can think of, beginning with that letter, within one minute. It is up to you to be the timekeeper—or you may want to enlist the help of a scorekeeper assistant. Suppose you name "H." As soon as you are ready to start, say "Go!" and the person designated will start pouring out words beginning with "H," like "hat," "heaven," "hold," "hemp," etc. Keep a word count and at the end of a minute, stop him. When time is called, select another letter, and the same thing takes place.

Too many people and you still want to play? Set up teams, designate a word-master for each of them, and pit team against team.

Hints and tips: Use a one-minute egg timer for accuracy.

Name of the game: The Rose

Type: Table contest.

  # of players: Small group

Supplies: A fresh rose; pencil and paper for the leader; light squares of netting and ribbon.

Formation: Casual seating at a table.

Object of the game: To guess correctly.

Play action: Pass around a fresh rose and let everyone enjoy its fragrance. When the rose comes back, ask your guests to guess the number of petals in the flower. (Keep a tally of their guesses.) Pick off each petal, counting as you go. The closest number

gets a prize. Place the petals in a small square of netting and tie them up with ribbon. These mini-fragrance sacs can be given away.

Hints and tips: Use more than one rose depending on the number of guests. Estimate one rose for every six people.

Name of the player: Wait a Minute

Type: Table game.

Supplies: Playing cards.   **# of players:** 4 to 6

Formation: Players in circle, round the table.

Object of the game: To be the first to get rid of your cards.

Play action: Deal out all cards. Each has its own number values. 1 = Ace, 11 = Jack, 12 = Queen, 13 = King. In the middle of the table, the starter puts down one or more cards facedown, declaring "Number One." He may be bluffing. ("Are they really ones?" you wonder.) Neighbor follows by putting on top one or more other cards, saying "Number Two." This continues all the way up to 13 or the king. If players still have cards, the game is not over, and Number One is started again.

At any point in play, any player may cry, "Wait a Minute!" The one who suspects a bluff uncovers whatever card or cards have just been put down, in order to check. If the suspicion was right, the bluffer is compelled to take *the entire pile* from the middle of the table. If the interrupter was wrong, he or she gets the whole pile.

Name of the game: Table Wares

Type: Table game.   **# of players:** Any

Supplies: Table with these actual objects on it; provide copies of the list with only the answers on it (see below), one for each player; prize.

Objects:	Answers:
onion	Hidden tears
last year's calendar	Bygone days
a nail in a block	A drive through the wood
scissors	We part to meet again
tacks on a box of tea	Tax on tea
iron on top of a shoe	Flat foot
alphabet	The greatest bet ever made

an old shoe	Wayworn traveler
Objects:	**Answers:**
small pile of dirt	My own native land
a candle	Light of other days
broken dish	Ruins of China
a candy heart, broken	Broken heart
sixteen pieces of candy	Sweet sixteen
four spices	The four seasons
hairpins	Pin-ups

Formation: Place objects on a table near the room where party is held. Guests enter and examine the table wares.

Object of the game: Each person tries to guess the correct matches to the objects. First player finished wins a prize.

Play action: Players have sheets of paper on which the answers are written. They must match these terms with the actual objects.

Name of the game: Prophecies
Fun to play at New Year's Eve parties.

Type: Table game.   **# of players:** Small group

Supplies: Place three cups on a table. One should be half full of milk, the second half full of water, and the third half full of vinegar; blindfold.

Formation: Players seated around a table. One guest is blindfolded.

Object of the game: Your fortune predicted.

Play action: A player is blindfolded and asked to touch one of the cups. The guest must then dip a finger into the first cup touched. If it contains milk, the life will be happy and he/she will marry (if already married, his/her life will be fruitful). If it contains water, a single blessedness will last for one or more years. If it contains vinegar, the wife or husband will cause much trouble.

Name of the game: Pea Pick

Type: Table game.   **# of players:** 6–8

Supplies: Cups, saucers, wooden matches, dried peas.

Formation: Seated around a table

Object of the game: First one to finish, wins.

Play action: In front of each player are a cup and saucer and two wooden matches. Inside the saucer are 12 dried peas or navy beans. At a starting signal, each begins lifting peas from the saucer to the cup using two matches. The first to move all the peas into the cup wins.

Hints and tips: Peas must not be touched, except by the matches.

Adaptation: Add this to other table relays for a longer event.

Name of the game: Resolutions (New Year's)

Type: Special table game.   **# of players:** Any

Supplies: Pencil and paper.

Formation: Seated at table or in circle.

Play action: Each guest writes down a New Year's Resolution, for example "lose weight," turns the paper down, and passes it to a neighbor two places to the left. The next item each guest writes down is the reason for the resolution, for example, "to keep peace." Pass papers again two places to the left, and this player reads the results.

Hints and tips: Phrase the resolution sentence like this: "I am going to___" "Because" (or, "In order to") "___."

Name of the game: Penny Pitching

Type: Table game.   **# of players:** One long table of players

Supplies: Chalk diagram of a target; supply of pennies; prizes.

Formation: Place the circle target about the size of a dessert plate at one end of a long table (about 9 feet or 3m); 6 players line up at the other end.

Object of the game: To lay pennies in the middle of the target for the most points.

Play action: Competitors flip pennies along table. Each player should have at least three chances—trying for the highest score.

Hints and tips: You may want to make another circle, like a bull's-eye, by drawing around a cup; mark different values for landed pennies.

Name of the game: Blindfold Cards

Type: Table game with cards.   **# of players:** Couples

Supplies: Playing cards; large table with chairs; blindfold; timer.

Formation: A couple is seated at each end of the table.

Object of the game: To collect the most cards.

Play action: One player of each couple is blindfolded. At a signal, the blindfolded player picks up cards, which are spread out all over the table, one at a time. He/She hands these to an encouraging partner who will give him/her hints about where to locate cards, but cannot touch or help him/her in any other way. Leader will call time—about 45 seconds for quick play.

Hints and tips: This could be run as a team game.

Adaptation: You do the scoring with the point totals of each card—Aces worth 1 only, Jacks 11, Queens 12, and Kings 13.

Name of the game: Rude Remarks

Type: Cards and thinking.   **# of players:** Small circle of close friends

Supplies: Two decks of playing cards.

Formation: Relaxed seating.

Object of the game: Absurd conversation.

Play action: A pack of cards is dealt out, two cards for each player. The leader holds in his hands a corresponding deck. He makes a personal insulting remark while, at the same time, turning up a card. The player holding the corresponding card tosses it on the table, and the remark given is applied to *him!* The offended person then carries on the game by making another insult. The leader turns up another card, and finds another "mark." The game continues until all the cards are used up.

Examples of remarks:
- He/She belongs in Hollywood as a character actor. When he/she shows character, he's/she's acting.
- He/She claims he's/she's just turned 35. Everybody wonders from which direction.
- He/She can talk 50% faster than anybody can listen.
- He/She gets his/her exercise watching TV horror movies and letting his/her flesh creep.
- She/He could have the last word even with an echo.
- She/He has a strange growth on her/his neck—her/his head.
- She/He looks worse than her/his passport photograph.

- She's/He's one person who would make a perfect stranger.

This is best suited for a small group of players who will enjoy a quiet, thoughtful time together. It is good for families to play also.

Name of the game: Speech Class
Type: Quiet thinking. **# of players:** Small group
Supplies: List of subjects; hat; timer.

Formation: Center for speaker, others casual seating.

Object of the game: To give a one-minute impromptu speech.

Play action: Player draws a subject out of a hat and talks for one minute on the topic.

Ideas for topics could include:
- Is routine demoralizing?
- What does "a sense of humor" mean to you?
- What is the difference between education and culture?
- Can charm be learned?
- What event in history would you have loved to witness?

- Do men do enough housework?
- Is admiration of modern or abstract art "faked"?
- What are the three most admirable qualities in a wife/husband?
- Tell us about different varieties of courage.
- Does science and its inventions add to our happiness?
- Are movies good for children?

And so on . . .

8.
RELAYS, MUSICAL ACTIVITIES, AND STUNTS

Extraordinary how potent cheap music is.
—NOEL COWARD, *PRIVATE LIVES*

ACTIVE GAMES AND RELAYS

Active games are best for casual get-togethers, where people are dressed informally. They are often played at picnics, barbecues, or other functions where there is lots of room. These activities can call for running, tagging, dodging, and throwing, which usually involve physical team play. Some active games can be played indoors or outdoors with some crossover into both categories. Active games are popular with all ages; don't hesitate to try them.

Relays need not be difficult to be fun. They are usually simple tasks everyone is capable of doing, but it is the team camaraderie, coupled with a fast time element, that makes the events challenging and full of mirth.

String a series of simple relays together for exuberant action. The multiple and varied tasks help to keep the participants moving, and there is the added excitement of team members urging each other on.

Note: For games with "It" or a leader: If the group is taking turns being either the leader or It, four or five changes in leadership or It are about right. Groups of five couples, or pairs, with five changes in leadership, lend themselves to a well-paced activity length. With larger numbers, the people in the team often get tired of waiting for their turn.

Name of the game: Passing Beans
Type: Team relay.   **# of players:** Teams
Supplies: Ten beans for each team; chairs.
Formation: Chair at one end of each team row.
Object of the game: First team to get all ten beans back is the winner.
Play action: Beans are placed on a chair. These are picked up, one

at a time, by the first player, and passed down the line using right hands only. When a bean reaches the end of the line, it is returned behind the players' backs, using left hands only.

Name of the game: Balloon Bang

Type: Team relay. **# of players:** Any, in teams

Supplies: Balloons, chairs.

Formation: Team line-ups.

Object of the game: To finish first.

Play action: First player blows up a balloon, ties it, and sits on it until it pops. This is repeated by the Number Two player until one team finishes.

Hints and tips: The second player cannot start until he hears a pop.

Adaptation: You can use a small paper bag instead of a balloon.

Name of the game: Hoops

Type: Team relay.   **# of players:** Any, in teams

Supplies: Hoops (hula-hoops), one for each team.

Formation: Team in order, long rows.

Object of the game: Complete team action first.

Play action: Each player in turn passes a hoop over his or her body, steps out, and passes it on.

Hints and tips: String a series of relay activities together.

Adaptation: Pass a balloon or basketball backward over the head, down the line from player to player. Then, pass it back between all feet through the row to the front.

Name of the game: It's Cold Out

Type: Team relay.   **# of players:** Teams

Supplies for each team: A hat, scarf, and large-sized gloves.

Formation: Competitors sit in chairs, one behind the other, in teams

Object of the game: To have all dress and undress and be the team to finish first.

Play action: First player puts on a hat, a scarf, and gloves, runs around the chairs, and hands these pieces of clothing to Player Number Two, who does likewise.

Name of the game: Balloon Tennis   ,

Type: Active outdoor.   **# of players:** Two teams small group

Supplies for each team: A tennis racket, balloon, and hoop.

Formation: Two teams are lined up and an assistant is holding a hoop a short distance away.

Object of the game: For each player to make a basket and be the first team to finish.

Play action: The first person picks up a tennis racket and a balloon. He/she pats the balloon gently, while heading toward the hoop. He/she needs to push it through, catch it, and return it to the next player, using only the racket, no hands.

Hints and tips: You can create hoops using the wire from an old lampshade, or you can use a round plastic basket with the bottom cut out.

Adaptations: Can't create a hoop? Modify the game by having the balloon go into a basket of any type. Your assistant can then take it out and hand the balloon back to the player to continue the relay.

Name of the game: Cork in Circle   **# of players:** Two small teams

Now you can use the corks you've been saving in the kitchen drawer!

Type: Active outdoor/team contest.

Supplies: Masking tape; large cork; tennis balls; smooth surface.

Formation: Create a fairly good-sized circle and a smaller inner circle with the tape. Two teams stand at opposite sides of the circle.

Object of the game: To knock the cork out of the circle.

Play action: Each side takes a turn at trying to whack a cork out of the circle by throwing a tennis ball at it. One point for the cork passing out of the inner circle; two for passing the outer line.

Hints and tips: Practice this ahead of time to determine the best size for your circles.

Name of the game: Cinderfella

Type: Team relay.   **# of players:** Teams of couples

Supplies: Bogus shoe pairs.

Formation: Split players evenly into teams. Men are seated in chairs, women standing behind them.

Object of the game: To be the first team to finish.

Play action: All the men's shoes are collected and put into a large pile. (Odd and intentionally "bogus" pairs are added.) On a signal from the "prince," women run to the pile and retrieve the correct shoes, return, and shoe partner, tie laces, etc.

Adaptation: Cinderella. Collect all the women's shoes, mix in bogus shoes, and proceed as before with the men running to the pile.

Name of the game: Subway Jam

Type: Relay contest.   **# of players:** Teams—men versus women

Supplies: Jumbled newspapers (all in disarray); sheets turned upside down and wrong order, one for each player.

Formation: Two rows of chairs facing each other.

Object of the game: Arrange newspapers in their correct order. First team to do it wins.

Play action: Men and women sit facing each other, knees touching, with no space left between, must put papers in order. Lots of rustle and hustle.

Name of the game: Potato Relay

Type: Active relay.   **# of players:** Any

Supplies: Potatoes; long nylon women's stockings; lightweight rubber balls, all the same size; trash cans; belts; chalk.

Formation: Divide players into teams; establish a goal line.

Object of the game: To knock the ball into the goal.

Play action: The belt is attached around the waist of the first player on each team. A potato is put inside the stocking, tied to the belt, and hung down the back of the player (potato should hang about 2" [5cm] from the floor). By swinging the potato between the competitor's legs, he or she must knock the ball into the goal—the trash can lying on its side.

Hints and tips: This event is *truly hilarious*—have a camera ready. Also, you might want to have two belts for each team—this gives the next-in-line time to "suit up."

Name of the game: Pea and Spoon

Type: Team relay/indoor or outdoor.

# of players: Any, in teams

Supplies for each team: Two saucers, one containing six peas, and a teaspoon; chairs.

Formation: Team line-ups.

Object of the game: To finish first.

Play action: On a "Go" signal, the first player picks up a spoon, and takes up one pea on it. The spoon is passed from team member to team member, until the last, who deposits it into a saucer. The spoon is them returned hand-to-hand to the front of the line for another pea. If the pea falls at any point, the player who dropped it must pick up the pea, go to the front of the line, and start again.

Name of the game: Sweet Spoon

Type: Team relay/indoor or outdoor.

# of players: Teams, any size

Supplies: Teaspoons for everyone; lumps of sugar; chair.

Formation: Players are seated in two rows facing each other. Each has a teaspoon *in his or her mouth.*

Object of the game: To be the team to finish the task first.

Play action: The player seated at one end is given a lump of sugar. He places this in the spoon and gently tips it into the spoon of his neighbor, who then does the same with the next team member. Should the sugar fall, it remains, and a new sugar cube is started at the beginning of the line.

Hints and tips: Use plastic spoons. Assistants may want to quickly retrieve the dropped cubes once play is begun again.

Good for kids, too!

Adaptation: With a toothpick in the mouth, try passing a lifesaver. (Only for good friends!)

Name of the game: Peanut Carry-on

Type: Team relay/indoor or outdoor.   **# of players:** Teams

Supplies for each team: Peanuts in shell; 2 butter knives; 2 small bowls; timer.

Formation: Team players standing in line.

Object of the game: To transport the most items.

Play action: On a signal, the first player is given a knife and places as many peanuts on it as possible. Then he/she carries them to a bowl across the room. Each player does likewise. After about five minutes, play stops. Count the peanuts in each bowl to determine the winning team.

Hints and tips: Should a peanut or peanuts fall, that player returns with an empty knife.

Name of the game: Blind Postal Clerk

Type: Active game.   **# of players:** 10–20

Supplies: Prepared slips, each with the name of a city; a master list of all the cities used for the leader; blindfold; chairs.

Formation: The group sits on chairs in a circle. One player, the Postal Clerk, is blindfolded and stands in the middle of the circle. The leader, standing just outside the circle, is Postmaster General and holds the master list of cities.

Object of the game: Not to lose your seat.

Play action: All seated players are given a slip of paper with the name of a city on it. The leader calls out two cities on the list. These people must immediately rise and exchange seats. The Blind Postal Clerk will try to catch them, touch them, or sit in one of the empty chairs. The player left without a chair will become the new Blind Postal Clerk. Players can jump, dodge, or run to escape, but they are not allowed to go outside the circle.

Hints and tips: If the Postal Clerk is having difficulty, the leader may call out a number of cities at one time. The fun is in having a player get caught, so sometimes the group will spontaneously try to help the Blind Postal Clerk. Pick a blindfold that is easy to get on and off.

Adaptations: This game can be altered to suit a theme. For a Christmas party, the slips of paper can contain holiday words instead of cities, such as Prancer, Santa, Holly, etc.

Name of the game: Balkan Dodge Ball

Type: Active outdoor.   **# of players:** Any, best with teams

Supplies: 2 volleyballs; under-inflate them for safety purposes.

Formation: Form two teams of approximately equal size. Each team lines up on either side of a center line. Playing area should be about the size of a badminton court.

Object of the game: To win by sending opposing team members to prison.

Play action: One player of each team starts a ball and plays it as in dodge ball, attempting to hit a player on the opposite side. A player may dodge it or catch it on the fly. If he catches it, he may play the ball, but if he fumbles or if the ball hits him or touches him in any way, he must go to prison. The prison zone is *behind* the opposing team's playing area. After a ball is played, it belongs to the opposing team for the next throw. The only exception is when a player throws a fly ball to one of his own teammates; then a player in prison may catch the fly ball and throw it into the opposing team's area. If a player is hit by this throw, the prisoner is free to go back to his own team's playing court.

Hints and tips: Being a prisoner can be an advantage if you are quick to capitalize on passes. This can be fast and furious fun.

Name of the game: Balloon Bomb

Type: Active outdoor.   **# of players:** 6–30 (even numbers)

Supplies: Good-quality balloons filled with water.

Formation: Everyone finds a partner. Players stand facing their partners in two rows—about three feet apart.

Object of the game: To be the two remaining partners.

Play action: At a signal, one line of partners tosses their balloons to their partners in the other row. Everyone is then instructed to take a step back, and the balloons are returned. This procedure is repeated as many times as necessary. A couple is eliminated when their balloon breaks.

Hints and tips: The less water in the balloon, the longer it will last. This is great for a hot summer day.

Name of the game: Cushion Touch

Type: Active indoor.   **# of players:** Large party, large room

Supplies: A large cushion or ottoman (a beanbag chair will do); lively music.

Formation: Large circle, all holding hands firmly; cushion in center.

Object of the game: Not to touch the cushion, but make your neighbor touch it.

Play action: Players swirl around trying to make their neighbors touch a cushion, while avoiding it themselves. As players touch it, they drop out.

Hints and tips: This is a raucous game. *Good for youngsters.*

Name of the game: Ping-Pong Baseball

Type: Active game/indoors   **# of players:** 8–20
    in a gym or large playroom.

Supplies: Ping-Pong balls; rolled-up newspaper bats.

Formation: Teams line up, as for a baseball game, with one team in the field and one team at bat.

Object of the game: To get the highest score.

Play action: There are no strikes; the ball must be hit or you are out. Game is played and scored like any regular baseball game.

Hints and tips: Handling the equipment makes for laughs. Have extra Ping-Pong balls on hand.

Name of the game: Bombard It

Type: Active game.   **# of players:** 12

Supplies: 10 beanbags; 12 plastic bottles.

Formation: Two teams of 6 players. Players line up within their own playing area (about the size of a badminton court). A center line (chalk or tape) divides the two teams. Six bottles are lined up, along the back, just inside each team's base line. Each team has 5 beanbags.

Object of the game: The first team to knock out all the opponent's bottles wins. You may choose a designated length of time to play instead.

Play action: On a signal, the players throw their beanbags into the opponent's area trying to knock down their bottles. A player may catch or block a beanbag in any way to prevent his team's bottles from going down. A bottle is considered out of the game if knocked over by a beanbag, or pushed over the base line by a beanbag or a player. Out-of-bound bags are put back into play by an assistant, who tosses them toward the forward line.

Hints and tips: A rough-and-tumble game, but beanbags are not dangerous. Suggest that players use chest-level or lower throws.

MUSICAL ACTIVITIES

Some activities lend themselves to music. These games usually require it. The possibilities for adaptation are endless and, yes, they are just as much fun as you remember they were when you were a child.

Name of the game: Pass the Package

Type: Music.   **# of players:** Any

Supplies: Small gifts wrapped in many layers and in many different boxes; music.

Formation: Players seated in a circle.

Object of the game: To keep the gift.

Play action: Package is passed to music. When the music stops, the person holding the package begins unwrapping it. But when the music starts again, he must pass it on *immediately*. The last player to finally get the wrapping off keeps the gift.

Hints and tips: Get two or more gifts going simultaneously for larger gatherings.

Name of the game: Bigamy

Type: Active/music.   **# of players:** 20+ large group

Supplies: Chairs; music.

Formation: Chairs in sets of 3, arranged in a circle formation.

Object of the game: To secure another "wife."

Play action: This is an interesting variation of Musical Chairs. Men sit in the middle of the three grouped chairs, with a "wife" on each side. There is one exception—one of the men has only one wife—and an empty chair. When the music starts, this man takes his present wife by the hand, runs across the circle, and grabs another man's wife. This player, finding himself with only one wife, does the same thing. When the music stops, the last 3 players to be tapped for a wife leave, taking 3 chairs away with them. The last remaining full family of three are the winners.

Hints and tips: Good for a dance club or music group in a large room.

Name of the game: Musical Pack

Type: Music/cards.   **# of players:** Any

Supplies: Deck of playing cards; rubber band; music; chairs.

Formation: Sitting in a circle.

Object of the game: Collect cards; prize.

Play action: A rubber band holds the cards secure, and the pack of cards is passed around to music. Each time the music stops, the player holding the pack takes 2 cards. When the cards are all used up, players total up their points. Aces are worth one point, Jacks 11, Queens 12, and Kings 13. The highest total wins.

Hints and tips: Toward the end, you can suggest "one card only."

Name of the game: Musical Chairs Not Removed

Type: Musical chairs.   **# of players:** Large party

Supplies: Chairs; music.

Formation: Chairs face outward in a circle, one for each player.

Object of the game: To be the last to have to remain seated.

Play action: This is different from the original musical chairs in that chairs are not removed. The game begins by all taking seats. Each player memorizes his position. Music starts, they get up and move clockwise. When the music stops, players have to carry on in the same direction until they reach their own chairs. Last one seated must sit for the rest of the game.

Hints and tips: Have an assistant act as referee to call out who exactly was last.

Adaptations: The game can be varied by going in the opposite direction, or by asking players to hop.

For stunt or additional game: Players who drop out early have to walk around the room to music with a book balanced on their head. When the music stops, they must go down on one knee. If the book falls, they are out for good. You will find some players who are experts.

Name of the game: Musical Pairs

Type: Musical chairs.   **# of players:** Large party

Supplies: Large room; chairs; music.

Formation: Single chairs, well spaced, about the room, one chair per couple, less one.

Object of the game: To secure a chair.

Play action: Played as couples, woman sits on man's knee. One pair of players has no chair. At the music's start, the couples walk in, out, and around the chairs. When the music stops, each man sits with his partner on his knee. The unseated couple is removed along with another chair of their choosing. Play for a designated amount of time; on the ending bell, the final unseated couple should do a forfeit (see page 114).

Adaptations: Man is blindfolded, led by partner.

Name of the game: Musical Pass

Type: Music.   **# of players:** Large party

Supplies: Large room; walking stick; music.

Formation: Players in circle.

Object of the game: To pass the stick.

Play action: Stick is passed to music. When music stops, the player holding the stick is eliminated.

Hints and tips: You will see players trying to throw the stick away.

Adaptation: Add a tap before the stick is passed.

Adaptation: Use a flashlight instead of a stick—and turn out the lights!

Name of the game: Musical Envelopes

Type: Music.   **# of players:** Large party

Supplies: 6 to 8 envelopes, each holding a different stunt or penalty; music.

Formation: Circle formation, standing up.

Object of the game: Who will "pay the Piper"?

Play action: An envelope is passed to music. When the music stops, the person holding it keeps it. The music starts again and another envelope is passed. When all are disposed of, the players who kept them step forward (one at a time), open and read the envelopes, and carry out the instructions inside.

Adaptation: A letter prepared earlier–and a gift. Once the music starts, the package is passed in one direction, and the letter moves in the opposite one. When the music stops, the player holding the letter is out. At the end, when you are down to two players, the winner–the one holding the package–opens the gift. The player holding the letter opens and it reads, "Nice try. Bow to the winner."

Name of the game: Musical Groups
Type: Music.   **# of players:** Large group
Supplies: Large room; music.
Formation: All move around in pairs.
Object of the game: Not to be left out.
Play action: Players move to the music. When the music stops, the leader calls out, "Fives!" Then, players scurry to get into a group of five. Odd ones are out. The next time the music stops, another number is called out . . . reducing finally to one.
Adaptations: Musical Island. Distribute pieces of cardboard of various sizes around the floor. When the music stops, players must crowd onto the cardboard. (One foot is permissible). If anyone's foot is touching the ground–that player is gone! A cardboard island is removed each round. Careful–these can be slippery, so you might want to play this on grass.

STUNTS AND FORFEITS

These are a great change of pace. The best players will often be people whom you know to be good sports. Forfeits and stunts are great fun with nary a minute for humiliation, and guests must never be the butt of a joke. Stunts are also fun for the other guests to watch, but it is up to you to make this a positive experience for all. Usually "victims" get so much attention, they wind up having as much fun as the audience. Although stunts may use only a few people in the action, they can involve the audience by letting them provide an accompaniment—clapping, cheering, giving encouragement, or sound effects. One enticing "high-interest-for-all" forfeit is to require the loser to pay a compliment to each guest.

Name of the game: Barnyard, Competition
Type: Stunt.   **# of players:** Large party
Supplies: 4 chairs; a hard-boiled egg; and a practiced M.C. (Master of Ceremonies).
Formation: Send about 4 people out of the room; they are to return one by one when called for. Place two chairs side by side. Let Miss X sit in one of them. A third and fourth chair are placed several feet away, facing the first two.

Object of the game: The amusement of all.

Play action: When the first victim is called, ask her to be seated next to Miss X, and advise her that this is a competition to find out "who is best at imitating farm animals."

Next, our victim is asked by the M.C. to make a noise like a pig. She does this. "Very good. Now a cow." *(The M.C. motivates her with drama, making guests believe this is a viable contest.)*
"Good, a cat." *(Wait for performance.)*
"Okay, a farm dog. Yes, quite good." *(Make sure that the audience responds favorably to the sounds; solicit their enthusiasm.)*
"Now, make the noise of a hen when she is laying an egg." The victim does this and the M.C. asks her to try again, or if it's done exceptionally well, says, "Thank you, that's all. Now you can go over and sit in *that* chair," indicating one of the single chairs across from the others.

*While the victim is walking away, Miss X places an egg on the seat that the victim has just vacated. A moment or two after the victim sits, her eyes will fall upon the egg on her previous seat.

Hints and tips: I have played this numerous times and it is *the best!* You, the leader, may act as the M.C., and, of course, while the victims are sent to the other room, Miss X will be told of her duty of placing the egg, without alerting the victim. This is an extremely funny event that is good for about four repetitions, and you'll find that nobody minds "laying an egg"!

Name of the game: Your Task

Type: Forfeit for one player.   **# of players:** One victim

Supplies: Glass of water; a ladder; a cane; and a shortbread cookie.

Formation: Others will watch and then walk away (all are confederates).

Object of the game: To fool the "loser."

Play action: You, the leader, will tell the "loser" that he must redeem himself for his poor performance. To do this, he must complete a simple task. Hand him a glass half-filled with water. A helper places the glass of water up against the ceiling. The victim must place the cane under the glass and hold it tightly against the ceiling. Then he is told he must dance a little two-step and eat a cookie, all while holding the cane fast against the glass. The trick is that, after he's eaten the cookie, the audience becomes neglectful and walks away, leaving him holding the glass!

Hints and tip: You might want to use a sturdy plastic glass.

Name of the game: I Bequeath

Type: Forfeit stunt.   **# of players:** One victim; helpers

Supplies: Pencil and paper.

Formation: Casual seating; one "victim" leaves the room.

Object of the game: To create an unusual, entertaining *Last Will and Testament.*

Play action: The player sent from the room is told that his "lawyers" are going to compile a list of his assets (effects) and that when he returns, he will be asked how he would like his estate disbursed. Leader and "lawyers" then compile a list of things the "deceased" (victim) supposedly desires to leave along with odd instructions. The list, of about 12 items, should be amusing, containing things like:

A toupee	to keep him/her warm.
Love letters	so as not to alarm___(victim's wife, mate).
Chest hair	for grooming and display.
Elevator shoes	to help reach prosperity.

The items could relate to the interests, hobbies, or disposition of the victim. You get the idea.

When the absent member returns, the leader asks him, "To whom will you leave item number 1? How about item number 2?" And so on. Hopefully, he will name relatives, charities, or institutions, or he can say, "I'll have that buried with me," or any other such wishes (*advise him of his options.*)

The leader then reads the list of items, matching them with his designated recipients, along with the corresponding instructions. (Use a pattern similar to: "I, being of *un*sound mind and body, do hereby will and bequeath . . ."

. . . My___

To___

In the hopes that . . .

(Or,) and ask that he . . .

(Or,) on condition that he . . .

. . . My___

To___
(Because) of his kindness . . .)
Hints and tips: Cleverness wins out.

Name of the game: There's a Sucker Born Every Minute
Type: Forfeit and stunt combined.   **# of players:** Any
Supplies: A prepared list of suggestions and guests.
Formation: Room is divided into two teams, with space left near the leader for performing.
Object of the game: To get players to perform stunts.
Play action: Make the teams think that this is a competition. Leader stands in front and calls for objects to be produced from pockets, purses, and persons. Suggestions for things to collect are a wristwatch, class ring, scarf, pen or pencil, postage stamp, hair ornament, and so on.

In the next stage of the game, the leader says, "Who is the owner of this?" and holds up an article for claiming. Before the item can be returned, the owner must perform a stunt (appropriate to the player, please).
Examples:
• Sing a song as a child of five might do it.
• Pretend you have won first place in a beauty contest. Make your acceptance speech.
• Kiss four bare legs (chair's legs).
• Sell a car/computer to someone in the audience.
• A dramatic actress on board a cruise ship has just lost her lover. Give the speech she makes just before she throws herself overboard.
• If you could be anybody, or tell who you would be and why.
• Recite the months of the year–alphabetically.

Are there some budding actors, straight men, or crackpots in your group? Try some of these ideas:

Name of the game: Thread on Your Jacket
Type: Stunt.   **# of players:** 1 or more actors
Supplies: Spool of thread; needle.

Formation: Stunt man or woman mixing with group.

Object of the game: To fool the unsuspecting.

Play action: Certain guests are provoked by loose threads. To prepare, draw a needle and thread through a suit seam of one of the guests. Put the spool in the inside pocket and pull off the needle, so that the thread hangs loose, about an inch or so. Someone will instinctively seek to remove the thread, which cannot be picked off! As the guest pulls. the thread grows longer!

Hints and tips: Clip and let a newly arrived guest have a turn!

Name of the game: Blow It Out

Type: Forfeit.   **# of players:** Any

Supplies: Candle; matches; blindfold; victim.

Formation: Casual grouping.

Object of the game: To blow out the candle.

Play action: The victim is blindfolded in front of a lighted candle, spun around three times, and let loose. He is instructed to find the candle and blow it out. Stand back! Can others do it? Let them try.

Name of the game: Captain Hook and Walking the Plank

Type: Forfeit or stunt.   **# of players:** 1 "victim"

Supplies: A good-sized, wide board 5" (12.5cm) or more in width, placed about 3" or 4" (7.5 or 10cm) off the floor on concrete blocks; a large bowl or bucket filled with water; blindfold.

Formation: The "victim" is instructed that for one reason or other, he must "walk the plank." He sees the setup being assembled. He is watched by the others.

Object of the game: To fool the subject into believing he will get wet.

Play action: The victim is blindfolded. He is to "walk the plank"– a board placed a short distance off the ground with a bowl of water at the end. With some gentle assistance, he is led down the plank to the "sea." (The water bowl is removed before he reaches the end, but *his anticipation* of reaching the water is very interesting to the pirate crew watching.) Will he step off willingly into the sea?

Hints and tips: Gently slosh the water around for good measure.

Name of the game: Plea for the Life Jacket

Type: Forfeit.   **# of players:** Small group

Supplies: None.

Formation: Four to six players facing a group.

Object of the game: To come up with the best story.

Play action: Your chosen individuals have been on a ship and it is wrecked. Who will get the life jacket? Each victim states his case, claiming to be the most valuable member of the community.

Hints and tips: Audience votes for the best story. Encourage tall tales and elaboration.

Name of Game: Tongue Twisters

Type: Forfeit.   **# of players**: Any

Supplies: List of tongue twisters; prizes.

Formation: Casual seating.

Object of the game: To say difficult phrases without error.

Play action: Recite three times in quick succession; for player with the silver tongue—a prize!
- She threw the six fried fish in the fireplace.
- Is a newly appointed Royal Academician in a position to make a decision?
- Esau Wood's wood saw would saw wood as no other would saw wood.
- Twisting and turning, the twenty-two trampers tried to traverse the twelve ridges.
- Saturday's coal stocks soared.
- Helen always heats the iron hastily.
- Please screw through six thicknesses.
- I sniff shop snuff, you sniff shop snuff.
- Miss Elizabeth Thistlethwaite would often whistle as she used the thick brush with the stiff bristles.

Name of the game: The Newspaper Couple

Type: Forfeit for a couple.   **# of players:** 1 couple

Supplies: One sheet of newspaper.

Formation: One couple tries positions.

Object of the game: To find a solution.

Play action: The couple is given a newspaper sheet and told they must both stand on it—but they cannot *touch* each other.

Hints and tips: *Answer:* There must be a door between them.

Name of the game: Back-or-Front Drill

Type: Skit.   **# of players:** Small group

Supplies: Buttoned or zippered dresses or coats; Halloween masks of complete faces and hats.

Formation: Line of players in front of room.

Object of the game: Audience laughter.

Play action: Volunteer play-actors put on dresses or coats back to front. They cover the back of their heads with a mask, and don a large hat to cover any distracting elements. The leader brings his team into the room and lines them up. Of course, they walk in with masks forward, so they are walking backwards! Then, the leader conducts a drill: "Arms forward stretch" (they come forward only a little), and, "Arms backwards" (they swing back to an amazing extent). The greater the variety of orders, the better.

Hints and tips: Some practice will help. Heads don't need to be turned at a severe angle.

Name of the game: One-Minute Test   **# of players:** Individuals

Type: Forfeit competition.   and team captain

Supplies: Timer; prepared topics.

Formation: Casual seating.

Object of the game: Quick thinking exercise.

Play action: Each player has to call out in the space of one minute as many answers as possible. Time and score carefully.

Hints and tips: Ideas for questions:
1) White objects
2) Things that give off heat
3) Names of composers
4) Spices
5) Names of dress materials
6) Office supplies
7) Hometown street names
8) Parts of the body
9) Things that cut
10) Names of nursery rhymes
11) Names of songs
12) Things with wheels
13) Names of sports
14) Movie star names, etc.

Adaptation: Use pencil and paper.

9.
SHOWER AND PAIRING GAMES, HUNTS, AND EVENTS

We are all worms, But I do believe I am a glow worm.
—WINSTON CHURCHILL

SHOWER AND SHOWER ACTIVITIES

Today's showers are very creative, and there are many different kinds. The basic idea is to provide household items, tools, or gifts that will help the honorees get started on their new lifestyle choice—whether that means getting married, having a child, or doing either again.

Theme showers are especially interesting, and using a unifying concept allows for easier, more creative gift-buying. These events are usually built around a room, such as kitchen utensils, bedroom or boudoir gifts, or romantic honeymoon send-off packages. Whichever theme you choose, be sure to include games that will unite the guests, because they are often from different sides of the family. Yikes! Family relations are in your hands . . .

Name of the game: Vanity Table

Type: Shower.   **# of players:** Small group

Supplies: Wooden bread board.

Formation: Seated in a circle; one player in the middle.

Play action: Each player is named after an object on a lady's vanity table. The person in the middle spins a round, wooden bread board and calls out, "Lipstick." The lipstick must catch the spinning board before it falls down. If she fails, she must perform a task, forfeit, or skill. If the player in the center calls out "Vanity," all players must change seats, and the odd one must pay a forfeit.

Hints and tips: Play until most everyone has had a chance to do something,

Name of the game: Just Five

Type: Shower or table game.   **# of players:** Small group

Supplies: Five beans on a plate or napkin at each place setting.

Formation: Guests seated for snacks, lunch, or conversation.

Object of the game: To direct and encourage conversation.

Play action: Guests are told that when they ask one another questions, anyone who is persuaded to answer with a direct "yes" or "no" is presented with a bean from the questioner's plate. The first guest to get rid of all 5 beans wins a prize.

Hints and tips: Use other items besides beans–Hershey kisses?

Name of the game: Hunt the Thimble

Type: Singing hunt.   **# of players:** Small group

Supplies: Thimble.

Formation: One player (the hunter) is sent out of the room. (This person could be the honored person or the shower recipient.)

Object of the game: To find the object.

Play action: When the hunter is called back into the room, he must

hunt for the thimble. The other guests must sing some song together. When the searcher gets nearer to the hidden object, their singing gets softer. When he/she gets farther away from the hidden object, it gets louder. The searches are guided entirely by modulation—until in silence the search is completed.

Hints and tips: Should your hunter fail—he/she may go out again, or select a different player.

Adaptation: Use songs with the shower theme.
Instead of a thimble, maybe a shower gift would be worth looking for.

Name of the game: Designers Surprise
Type: Wedding shower contest.   **# of players:** Small group
Supplies: A piece of paper inside a sealed envelope for each person, with his/her name on the front.
Formation: Casual seating.
Object of the game: Neatness counts!

Play action: Pass out the sealed envelopes with the paper inside. Tell your guests this is a race. At a signal, they are to open their envelopes and tear the paper inside into the form of a wedding cake.

Hints and tips: Collect all envelopes and present them to your honored guest. She gets to judge who wins—on the basis of neatness, trim and tidy appearance, and the careful way . . . *the envelope was opened!*

Name of the game: Only the Best of Friends
Type: Shower quiz.   **# of players:** Small group
Supplies: Pencil and paper; questions.
Formation: Circle of casual seating.
Object of the game: Funny answers.

Play action: Each guest is asked to write down four people of the opposite sex on their paper. These are passed to the person to the right, twice. The leader then asks four questions, which are answered by the names on the paper: 1) Who would you marry? 2) Who would you take as a lover? 3) Who would you want with you on a platonic cruise? 4) Who would you push off a cliff?

Hints and tips: Play two rounds. The first time, use the names of famous persons; the second time, use people you all know.

Name of the game: Match It

Type: Shower or sewing circle game.   **# of players:** Any

Supplies: Paper dolls with names to be matched with the articles printed on them (see the template for the doll on page 127); envelopes with straight pins, fabric swatches, and miscellaneous items to be matched.

Formation: 2 or 3 people per team sitting near each other, or at table.

Object of the game: To be the one having the most correct answers when time is called.

Play action: Each player (or team) is given a doll figure and an envelope containing pins and fabric swatches. At the signal, the players open their envelopes and begin to match the items with the titles on the figure.

Hints and tips: Suggestions for matched pairs:

1)	bride	lace
2)	storyteller	yarn
3)	fisherman	net
4)	lumberjack	corduroy
5)	banker	checked material
6)	newspaperman	black and white print
7)	shepherd	wool
8)	government worker	red bias tape
9)	fireman	nylon hose
10)	widow	black material
11)	naval officer	gold braid

Hints and tips: When making dolls, place the titles on each figure in different positions. Allow 6–10 minutes depending on how many are working together.

Name of the game: Family Reunion

Type: Shower game.   **# of players:** Small group

Supplies: Playing cards–or prepare index cards by writing or drawing different things or creatures on "four" on them, such as 4 cards with 4 tigers, 4 with 4 mice, 4 with 4 hats.

Formation: Players circulate.

Object of the game: To find the complete set or "happy family" of four.

Play action: Give each player one card out of the set. Place the

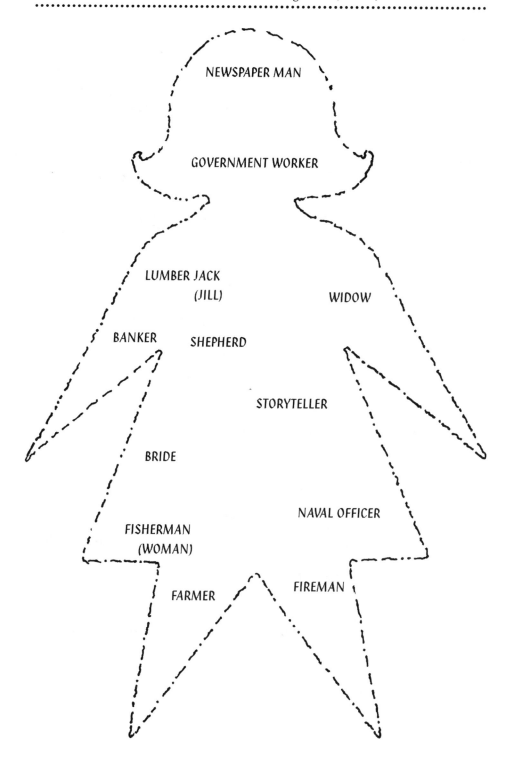

other three all around the room in different positions. The first player to assemble his set or "family " is the winner.

Adaptation: You can use the Ace, King, Queen, and Jack in all four suits, children's animal cards, baseball, or football cards. You can also adapt card selection or drawing to your theme.

Name of the game: Memory Book

Type: Shower game.   **# of players:** Small group

Supplies: A scrapbook that can be taken apart so each person can work on his or her own page; work table covered with oilcloth or similar material; bits and pieces of any sort of scrap material on hand:

construction paper	flowers
foils	sequins
brightly colored cellophane	postcards
buttons	women's magazines
pipe cleaners	actual photos
string	scissors
ribbon	Scotch tape
lace	

various types of glue (archival glue preferred)

Formation: Guests need plenty of elbow room around a work table.

Object of the activity: Everlasting memories.

Play action: Each guest needs to construct a page that evokes memories of her association with the honored guest. The participants can use the materials available and might want to bring some of their own photos or mementos. They can use poems, jingles, jokes, or captions to help with the creative endeavor. The finished product will be assembled and displayed. A lot of stories and laughter will result. The name of the author should go on the finished page.

Adaptation: Instead of a Memory Book, the finished pages can be put into open picture frames.
This activity is also good for a farewell party.

OTHER ODD EVENTS AND ACTIVITIES

Name of the game: Teach a Task

Type: Activity (planned).   **# of players:** Small group

Supplies: Whatever is needed for project. Make arrangements for supplies and instructions lists ahead of time.

Formation: Tabletop area for all.

Object of the activity: To learn a new skill.

Play action: Each guest has 5 to 10 minutes to teach a task.

Suggestion for activities:
- How to fold napkins into different shapes
- How to make a whirligig
- How to frost a cookie
- How to wrap a package
- How to change a tire
- How to write a complaint letter
- How to draw a cartoon

- How to make a safety pin bracelet
- How to tole-paint roses
- How to embroider, etc.

You will be surprised at how talented your guests are. This could turn into a monthly event.

MORE ACTIVITIES

- Have guests create their very own flags.
- Create decorative corsages: For a baby shower, you could make a giant corsage for the new mother. Roll a bib into a flower, attach a baby spoon, rattle, washcloth rolled into another flower; attach diaper pins, a "binky," etc.
- Fill balloons–with prize numbers, confetti, rice, small objects, puzzle pieces, etc., and then use the ingredients in the next game.

OTHER IDEAS FOR SPECIAL ACTIVITIES

Decorate a tree for Christmas or for the birds outdoors
Christmas caroling or baking cookies
Strawberry/watermelon festival–private version
Progressive dinners (appetizer at one home, salads at another,
    entree at a different address, etc.)
Cooking class
Make ice cream
Make ornaments, gifts, bazaar items
Teach a folk, square, round, or line dance
Poetry reading
Board game rounds
Quilting group (play word and thinking games)
View films
Make a video or movie
Bon Voyage or travel club get-together
Audubon or hiking event
Make a memory (scrapbooking)
Calendar play (find unusual days or special "weeks" to cele-
    brate, for example, Dick Clark's birthday National Maritime
    Day, full moon phase, etc.)
Water events: beach or pool party, canoe races, fishing contest
Party barge cruise
Buggy ride in the country

Community cleanup
Wine and cheese fete
Housewarming; new business ribbon cutting (have contests)
Crafts exchange
Arts festival (before or after an event)
Carnival with contests, juggling and music instruction, clown
    makeup, and mime training
Sleigh or hayride
Auction: auction off goods, lunches, or dates
Staged productions:
                    professional magic or infomercial
Portrait party: have camera, costumes, and props
Suppers: chili, spaghetti, pancakes
Luau party
Rush party

HUNTS

Hunts are a unique type of party entertainment—especially if you have a large house and you don't mind guests exploring it on their own. Squirrel away private papers or artifacts for security.

Name of game: Polaroid or Digital Camera Hunt

Type: Hunt.   **# of players:** Small teams

Supplies: Prepared assignment lists in checklist form, such as: a tombstone, a jogger or dog walker, grocery sackers, a policeman, a particular statue. Instant, digital, or Polaroid-type cameras; film, batteries.

Formation: Break into teams for a "hunt" using cameras and cars.

Object of the game: To return first with the most photo assignments completed.

Play action: Teams provide photographic proof of their visiting preselected locations.

Adaptation: Hunt for sounds using a tape recorder. Assignments for this list could include: a dog barking, a train whistle, a fast-food order, a chicken clucking, a bus, roller rink or bowling sounds, a waterfall, etc.

Hints and tips: Invitations can be made to look like a camera with the film rolling out, or like film rolled up in a small canister.

Name of the game: Cobweb Hunt   **# of players:** Small group
Type: Hunt or pairing game.   of couples
Supplies: One ball of twine or string for every two players.
Formation: Casual mixing.
Object of the game: To pair up a man and a woman as a couple in a game format.
Play action: To begin, the men are each given a ball of twine. They tie one end of the ball to a chair, table leg, or some other stationary object. Then, as they move about the room, they let the twine out, wherever they go. With a dozen people doing this, you can imagine that guests will be getting caught in the web. As soon as each man runs out of twine, he gives his end of the line to the host, and goes back to his starting point–where he tied the twine in the first place. After the host receives all the empty ball lines, he/she will distribute these ends, one to each woman present. Each woman then starts rolling up her twine, while the men begin winding their end from the starting point. When they meet each other, they are partners for another game.

Name of the game: New Business
Type: Contest hunt.   **# of players:** Small group
Supplies: Cards or pieces of paper made up in advance; hat; timer.
Formation: Players mixing, hunting.
Object of the game: To be the first to collect inventory and supplies for their new business.
Play action: Each player selects an occupation from a hat. Hidden around the room are small papers with items written on them that might be needed for their business. Players find as many items as they can in a given time.
Hints and tips: Items can be cut from magazines and pasted on cards.
Suggested businesses and items:
- *Hairdresser:* Combs, scissors, mousse, permanent solution, wigs, curling iron, dryers, setting lotion, hair clips, shampoo, hairspray, hair dye, rollers, etc.
- *Bakery:* Buns, bread, donuts, cakes, cookies, rolls, bagels, muffins, pies, French bread, bread sticks, coffee cakes, crusty breads, etc.

- *Florist:* Roses, vases, ribbon, florist wires, bulbs, ferns, carnations, fertilizer, tulips, florist block, baby's breath, silk flowers, green tissue, etc.
- *Sporting goods:* Football, helmet, tennis rackets, golf spikes, golf balls, racing shorts, bikes, soccer ball, bowling ball, athletic cup, canoe, catcher's mitt, golf clubs, etc.
- *Shoe store:* Heels, wingtips, boots, tennis shoes, polish, socks, shoe tree, nylons, sling-backs, slippers, suede bucks, hiking boots, pumps, etc.
- *Grocery store:* Milk, eggs, orange juice, potato chips, bananas, cereal, toilet paper, lunch meat, jelly, coffee, cheese, butter, lettuce, etc.
- *Stationers:* Pens, birthday cards, wrapping paper, calendars, envelopes, photo albums, postcards, tape, gift tags, address books, thank-you cards, notebooks, rubber stamps, etc.
- *Hardware store:* Hammer, nails, measure, pliers, pinchers, hose, vise, saw, sandpaper, bolts, locks, tacks, hooks, etc.

Hints and tips: You have the option of including the list of business supplies on the back of the occupational card or not. Obviously, it will be harder without them, so allow more time if you choose to play without lists.

Name of the game: Treasure Hunt

Type: Active indoor hunt.　　　　　　**# of players:** Large party

Supplies: Magazine pictures; cardboard; pencil and paper; prize.

Formation: Players go off on a hunt.

Object of the game: String clues together leading to the location of the prize.

Play action: Magazine pages (stiffened by pasting on cardboard) are placed around the room. *One item is circled on each page.* By taking the first initial of each, a word can be formed that will lead the seeker to the treasure. Word could be "laundry room," which would mean the magazine photos would be of Lipstick, Apple, Underwear, etc., and the items would all be circled in red marker. Green circled photos of Raisins, Old Taylor, etc., would be the hint for the second word "room."

Hints and tips: You can leave the prize in full view for easy play.

Name of the game: Treasure Hunt 2

Type: Active/indoor hunt.   **# of players:** Large party

Supplies: A word card for some players to wear; straight pins; pencils and paper for all; a prize for a team.

Formation: Split players into equal teams; mixing guests gather clues, then hunt for prize.

Object of the game: To locate all the individual words and then string them together in a sentence that tells where to find a treasure.

Play action: The words form a clue sentence. Words are pinned on several players' shirts or dresses. Everyone has paper and pencil. Players take note of the words until they have collected them all. Then, they arrange them to form a sentence that gives instructions for finding the treasure. For example, you might color-code words belonging to the same sentence, for example *"Prize is not in plain sight."* All six words in this first sentence would be **green**. The next sentence could be: *"The prize is downstairs"* with all the individual words in **red**. Another sentence could say: *"Washing machine"* in two **blue** words. Next, *"Look inside for clue"* all in **yellow** words. (Sixteen people will be wearing words if you use this pattern.) Then, a note *inside* the washing machine will say *"On child's bed!"* Have the prize sitting there.

Hints and tips: Players will be assembling the words first, unscrambling them, and then hunting.

Name of the game: Eternal Triangles

Type: Hunt and barter.   **# of players:** Any

Supplies: Old pack of playing cards, cut diagonally into 4 triangles; timer; prizes.

Formation: A mixing hunt.

Object of the game: To collect the most complete cards.

Play action: On a signal, tell your guests in which rooms the cards are hidden and let them go hunting. When you think they have had enough—perhaps three to five minutes or so—collect them into one room to see how many complete cards have been found by each person—this does not necessarily mean the greatest number of pieces.

Hints and tips: The shape of the pieces make them easy to hide;

under throw rugs, in door crevices, folds of curtains, behind pictures, between leaves of books, under vases (leave a corner slightly visible). Encourage guests to barter with each other for the missing pieces by calling out their requirements.

Adaptation: Walk around and surreptitiously replace pieces that have been taken with some you have left.

Name of the game: Hunt the Pairs

Type: Hunt.   **# of players:** Any

Supplies: Cocktail sticks, cuff links, stamps, corks, earrings, hair clips, screws, nuts, washers, coins, nails, beads, buttons, matches, beans, aspirin; envelopes.

Formation: Guests move around.

Object of the game: First to complete the task wins. (Give prize for first, and forfeit for last.)

Play action: Before the party, conceal over as wide an area of the house as possible a variety of small articles. The whole of each article need not be visible as long as part of it can be seen. Prepare as many envelopes as you have guests by placing in each about a half-dozen items that are partners to the hidden ones. Give one envelope to each guest and ask him/her to find the corresponding article.

Hints and tips: If an aspirin has a cross on it, another with a cross is required to complete the pair. You can have more than one pair of the same article by marking them differently. Use paint markers, flags, ribbon, or other tools to differentiate items.

Name of the game: Animal Crackers

Type: Noisy hunt.   **# of players:** Small group

Supplies: Ruled paper with approximately 25 squares and a different animal's name at the top of each; pencils; gifts; food for animals, such as peanuts in the shell, wrapped candies, etc.—25 for each player, hidden around the house (only one can be taken from each spot).

Formation: Guests hunt for "food." People may have to stretch or bend to discover objects, but should not move anything.

Object of the game: First form filled out wins.

Play action: Players get a form and a pencil. They put their name at the top. From then on, the only sound they can make is the one made by the animal listed on their form. They hunt for "food"—which can be peanuts, pretzel nuggets, or candy. When they find an object, they do not touch it, but point with their nose and make their animal noise to attract your attention. You collect the object and initial one square on their form for each food item found.

Hints and tips: Use an assistant or two. This will get noisy and just plain ridiculous. Be sure the animal's cry can be imitated.

Animal suggestions: Dog, owl, wolf, cuckoo, sheep, donkey, hen, pig, cow, horse, bird, turkey, cat, duck, chicken, lion.

Name of the game: Big Lucky Letters

Type: Hunt.   **# of players:** Small group

Supplies: Small colored papers, each with a different letter; timer; prizes or treats.

Formation: Players hunt, then they meet.

Object of the game: To collect a lot of points.

Play action: On a signal, players collect hidden letters. They do not know their value. When you call "time," they reassemble. Now, the scoring:
"B" for "best" is worth 10 points;
"S" for "second best" is equal to 5 points;
"A" is for "add," add 20;
"T" is for take away, which is minus 20;
"H" is a one-shot "Hoo-ray," equal to 25 (or 50, if you prefer).

Adaptation: Develop your own scoring system. You can have some dummy letters with no real points.

Hints and tips: Ten letters for each person should be about right.

Name of the game: The Mostest

Type: Outdoor area or garden hunt.   **# of players:** Pairs

Supplies: Timer; list; prizes.

Formation: Pairs are hunting on the grounds.

Object of the game: To find superlatives.

Play action: Players collect the biggest, the roundest, the brightest—

and bring them in for comparison. A point for the best of each.

Hints and tips:
1) The largest leaf
2) Brightest berry or flower
3) Smoothest pebble, stone, or shell
4) Longest blade of grass or stick
5) Thickest stem or twig
6) Blackest object, etc.

EVENTS

An entire party can be set up around one single "event." One such popular event would be a Mystery Night, which includes a lot of observation, cooperation with others in pairs or groups—however you decide to play it—and several different activities to choose from, so everyone can eventually interact with everyone else. Although event parties involve advance preparation, once it is set up and the play begins, the time will fly!

Here are a few new ideas for events that I hope you won't hesitate to use.

MYSTERY NIGHT

The game ideas that follow can be used to make up an entire mystery evening. You could pair two of these, or go all out and stage the complete set for your mystery-loving friends. There's something here for all those frustrated Sherlocks and Charlie Chans.

Name of the game: The Crime

Type: Mystery Night test.   **# of players:** Any, plus actors

Supplies: Pencil and paper; clock or watch; prepared questions.

Formation: Guests casually seated—unaware of action until it happens.

Object of the game: To get the most details correct.

Play action: You may want to hire some drama club members from a nearby college. Stage a pretend crime. One person can "steal" books off a shelf, remove a candlestick, or pretend to kill another. All the guests have now become eyewitnesses. Question each one, privately, in a separate interview. (Make sure they don't

compare notes.) After the questioning, bring everyone together for results.

Hints and tips:

Some questions you might ask:

What was the sex, race of the perpetrator?
Approximate age?
Height, weight, color of hair, eyes, complexion?
Any physical scars or marks?
Glasses? Facial hair?
Voice?
What was he/she wearing?
What did he/she do?

Name of the game: What Do You Hear?

Type: Mystery Night test.   **# of players:** Any

Supplies: Tape recorder and playback machine; pencils and paper; prize. Tape distinctive sounds or voices around your house, office, or community.

Formation: Casual seating.

Object of the game: To identify the most sounds.

Play action: Your sleuths are to identify the sounds they hear and write them down. The most correct answers wins a prize.

Some Sound Suggestions:

Flushing toilet	Any type of bell or signal
Washing machine	Door chime
Blender	Sandpaper
Cell phone	Voices (stars) off a film clip
Copy machine	

The possibilities are inexhaustible.

Name of the game: What Fabric Is This?

Type: Mystery Night test.   **# of players:** Any

Supplies: Swatches of fabrics or fibers taped to white index cards and numbered. Magnifying glass; good light; pencil and paper; prize. "Master list" of correct answers.

Formation: Guests casually seated, passing samples. (If you want to speed things up you can make two sample boards.)

Object of the game: To identify the fabric, most correct wins.

Play action: Players may touch fabrics, study under a magnifying glass.

Hints and tips: Some ideas:

Cotton, silk, wool, nylon, rubber, hemp, dryer lint, mohair, corduroy, etc.

Adaptation: Small squares of fabric that can be viewed under a microscope only.

Name of the game: Paper and Hard Evidence

Type: Mystery Night test.   **# of players:** Any

Supplies: Matches torn out of a matchbook; aluminum foil, waxed paper; pinked felt, etc. Number and catalog all samples.

Formation: Guests casually mixing.

Object: To identify the original source; just for fun!

Play action: Tear matches out of a matchbook, tear several foil papers, etc., in half (several of each type). Paper is made of wood fibers that have been pressed together. When you tear paper, the fibers separate and no two pieces of paper will tear the same. Your guests are to match the two halves; or link the unknown evidence to the original source as they would do in the lab.

Name of the game: Guess the Lip Print

Type: Mystery Night test.   **# of players:** Any

Supplies: Lipstick prints from a glass, and also from an index card; dark-colored construction paper.

Formation: Guests mixing and matching.

Object: Identify and match.

Play action: Compare the lip print made on the glass with that made on the index card. See how many the group can match correctly.

Name of the game: Fingerprint Identification

Type: Mystery Night test.   **# of players:** Any

Supplies: Ink pads; soap for cleanup; index cards; a glass; cocoa powder; talc; a soft brush; dark-colored construction paper.

Formation: Guests mixing and matching.

Object: Collect fingerprints and match.

Play action: Rub your finger alongside your nose to collect oil, then make your print. Use light-colored talc and an extra-soft paint brush to find prints against dark backgrounds. Lift the prints with clear tape; prints lifted with talc go on dark-colored construction paper. Use cocoa powder on prints made on light-colored or white backgrounds. After lifting the prints with tape, apply them to the index card. Test for prints on cardboard, foil, plastic bag, metal, etc.

Name of the game: City Tour Highlights

Type: Presentation of video clip   **# of players:** Any
   or photographs or slides.

Supplies: Take videotape or photos around your hometown. Photograph monuments, local sites, and attractions. Include pictures of unusual or unattractive areas as well.

Formation: Viewers seated for your narration.

Object of the game: Laughs and unsolicited comments.

Play action: You are conducting a "tour" of your city. Narrate the picture selections you have taken; plan to ham it up and have fun with some of the sites. For example, you could describe a shot of the local topless bar as "The Area's Great Nightlife." The local Wal-Mart could be referred to as "An Upscale Shopping Experience," etc.

Hints and tips: Wonderful for an event with a shorter time allotment, such as with a newcomer party or tea.

Name of the game: Crazy Airways

Type: Active, pencil-and-paper.   **# of players:** Up to 48

Supplies: Specially prepared player cards; "itinerary sheets" either hand-lettered or computer printed; pencil and paper; timer. The itinerary sheets should be put on posterboard (something fairly substantial), and each must be tacked at a different location in the room or in adjoining rooms, because people will congregate around the boards. The winning player will call out 48 city pairs—winding up in his own departure city—for checking against the full itinerary.

Formation: Players search for routings, going from location to location indoors.

Object of the game: Winner is the one who visits the largest number of cities in the time allotted, between 15 and 20 minutes. Prize for the first traveler to finish.

Play action: All players are making an air trip and flying the same route, but each starts off at a different point. On each player's card you will have written the name of a tour city with which to *begin* the journey. The player first locates his town on one of the itinerary sheets, say *London,* for example. When he finds *London,* the itinerary tells him the name of the town he must fly to next *(in this case it's Hull)*. He writes it down and goes in search of this new city. He finds it on another sheet and writes down the name of the next stop *(Hull to Amsterdam)*, and so on.

Hints and tips: This is an exciting hustle and search game.

Crazy Airways Itinerary Sheets (one of each):

Sheet # 1
London to Hull
Los Angeles to Mexico City
Aden to Durban
Colombo to Rangoon
Perth to Wellington
Paris to Venice

Sheet #2
Glasgow to Shetlands
Rangoon to Singapore
Anchorage to Vancouver
Montevideo to Dakar
Amsterdam to Brussels
Lisbon to Bordeaux

Sheet #3
Venice to Budapest
Winnipeg to Toronto
Brest to Southampton
Durban to Delhi
Hong Kong to Tokyo
Brisbane to Perth

Sheet #4
Mexico City to Havana
Hull to Amsterdam
Havana to Trinidad
Dunedin to Anchorage
Lima to Montevideo
Shetlands to Oslo

Sheet #5
Manila to Hong Kong
Quebec to Montreal
Cairo to Aden
Chicago to Los Angeles
Havana to Santiago de Cuba
Trinidad to Lima

Sheet #6
Delhi to Colombo
Tokyo to Brisbane
Jakarta to Manila
New York to Chicago
Southampton to Dublin
Budapest to Cyprus

Sheet #7
Brussels to Paris
Vancouver to Winnipeg
Bordeaux to Brest
Dakar to Madeira
Dublin to Glasgow
Oslo to London

Sheet #8
Toronto to Quebec
Cyprus to Cairo
Montreal to New York
Singapore to Jakarta
Wellington to Dunedin
Madeira to Lisbon

Hints and tips: This is a great activity for a travel club or a foreign exchange student party, and you can really have fun with the details. Hang travel posters, display artifacts from around the world, and serve exotic foods indigenous to foreign lands.

FORMING PARTNERS, GROUPS, AND TEAMS

Guests without partners will be shy about finding someone to play with—especially if all are strangers. The games that follow will solve that problem. The following devices for forming partners, groups, or teams may also be used as games themselves.

Name of the game: Similes

Type: Pairing or contest.   **# of players:** Any

Supplies: Cards prepared ahead of time, as many as you have guests. Half of them have the first part of the simile; the other half have the other. See examples below.

Formation: Players mingle.

Object of the game: To find the other half of the simile.

Play action: Half the players are given a "first part" simile card, and the others are given the words that complete it. They need to match up the two parts to make a complete saying.

Examples:

Happy as . . . a lark	Blind as . . . a bat
Sly as . . . a fox	Poor as . . . a church mouse
Limp as . . . a rag	Fleet as . . . a hare
White as . . . snow	High as . . . a mountain
Cold as . . . ice	Hard as . . . a rock
Sick as . . . a dog	Sour as . . . a lemon
Stiff as . . . a poker	Neat as . . . a pin
Black as . . . ink	Ugly as . . . sin
Fit as . . . a fiddle	Flat as . . . a pancake
Clear as . . . crystal	Crazy as . . . a loon
Bright as . . . a new penny	Dry as . . . a bone
Mad as . . . a hatter	Sharp as . . . a tack
Playful as . . . a kitten	Thin as . . . a rail
Rare as . . . hen's teeth	Deep as . . . the ocean
Sweet as . . . honey	Tough as . . . shoe leather
Pretty as . . . a picture	Proud as . . . a peacock
Lively as . . . a cricket	Quick as . . . lightning
Smooth as . . . silk	Slippery as . . . an eel
Large as . . . life	Clean as . . . a whistle
Warm as . . . toast	Busy as . . . a bee
Wise as . . . an owl	Tight as . . . a drum

Adaptations: The answers can be hidden around the room, and the last player to find his match gets a forfeit.

Name of the game: Find Me

Type: Form couples.   **# of players:** Any

Supplies: Index cards, pencils; hat or basket.

Formation: Mingling for pairing off.

Object of the game: To find a partner.

Play action: Each female guest writes a description of herself and her clothing. The cards are mixed in a hat. Each man draws one and looks for the woman described.

Name of the game: Literary Pairs

Type: Form partners or book club activity.   **# of players:** Any

Supplies: Name tags made up ahead of time; pins.

Formation: Mingling for pair-off.

Object of the game: Bogus books look for their imaginary authors.

Play action: Name tags have the names of books on some, authors on others.

Hints and tips:
   Suggestions for titles and author:

1)	*The Open Cage*	Freda Bird
2)	*No Vintage Year*	M.T. Sellers
3)	*Yellow River*	I.P. Daley
4)	*Roaming*	Wanda Luste
5)	*Brilliant Future*	Rosie Times
6)	*Escaped Convict*	Wendy Leeve
7)	*World's End*	R.U. Ready
8)	*Henpecked*	Olive Mealone
9)	*Murder Plan*	Will E. Douitt
10)	*Monsoons*	Howitt Raines

Make up your own!

Adaptation: Use your theme idea for pairings. Having a *cooking class?* For pairs you could use:

Ham and eggs	Meat and potatoes
Pork and beans	Salt and pepper . . .

Adaptation: Match the Myth: match the names of mythical characters to their associations:

Midas	golden touch
Theseus	the Minotaur
Hercules	twelve labors

Sisyphus	rolling a stone up a mountain
Adonis	beauty
Aphrodite	love

Name of the game: Family Portrait

Type: Grouping ideas. **# of players:** Any, in sets

Supplies: Index cards with "family" names, one for each guest.

Formation: Guests mingle.

Object of the game: To divide guests into groups.

Play action: Say you want to divide your guests into groups of four. An amusing way of doing this is to invent sets of family names. Pass out the cards and let the guests do the rest.

Hints and tips: An example of family names for dividing groups into four:
- Colonel I.M. Murgatroyd
- Mrs. R.U. Murgatroyd
- Miss B. Murgatroyd
- and Izzy Murgatroyd

Further Tips

Here are some ideas to help you introduce guests to each other, and to get them interested in each other.

Post an *"At this Party"* sign. An example of this would be, "At this party is one entomologist, two bridge players, a professional photographer, an architect, a wild animal trainer," and so on, using the unique talents of your guests.

Have a *"Guest of Honor"*? Say the honored person is a doctor. Ask each of your guests to write out prescriptions for the guest; play games using medical terminology; create a game identifying doctor's tools and instruments; make a contest out of an anatomical quiz.

How well do you know your friends? Phone each guest before the party and ask them questions about their lives. Inform guests that this personal information will be used at the party. Maiden names, pets' names, strange adventure or vacations; where or how did you meet your spouse; most unusual job, first date, won a special award or honor?–things like that. Then, formulate questions around this personal trivia information and use for a quiz at the party.

Need a tiebreaker? Have several foreign phrases at the ready. If and when you have a tie, let them both take a shot at translating their phrases. The person who comes the closest wins.

For a skill tiebreaker: Draw a pattern for Nine Toss (below) either in chalk outside or on a large piece of posterboard and have the "tie" players toss a beanbag for the highest point(s).

1	9	4
5	7	2
3	8	6

10.
GIFT-GIVING GAMES

All charming people, I fancy, are spoiled. It is the secret of their attraction.
—OSCAR WILDE

Nothing brings out the party atmosphere in guests like knowing there is a little gift in store. The very best incentive for a game-player is still the prize at stake!

Name of the game: The White Elephant

Type: Gift-giving.　　　　　　　**# of players:** Any

Supplies: Guests bring the most useless, most ugly, most ridiculous gift they can find, wrapped beautifully.

Formation: Casual seating.

Object of the game: To find a gift you can live with.

Play action: As the host, you choose any gift and open it; everyone Oohs and Aahs. You then draw a name, and that person can either claim the first gift opened or find a new one. And so on . . .

Hints and tips: You can have a rule that a gift may be stolen from its recipient only twice—after that it is theirs!

Name of the game: Unique Find a Gift

Type: Gift or prize hunt..　　　　**# of players:** Small group

Supplies: Good-weight string, prizes, scissors; a fairly large room.

Formation: Players mix.

Object of the game: To uncover a small prize or gift.

Play action: Cut long pieces of string and tie a small prize to the end. Hide the prize from immediate sight, but wind the string carefully (not tightly) around, in, and out of objects–around the legs of chairs, for example. The strings can look like a messy spider web. Strings should begin at a common starting point. Players unravel the string until it takes them to the prize.

Hints and tips: Expect a lot of crisscrossing and laughter.

Name of the game: Whose Gift?

Type: Gift-giving.   **# of players:** Any

Supplies: Gifts, brought by other guests or your own offerings; advance preparation for packaging.

Formation: Guests seated.

Object of the game: Create clever, distinguishing gifts.

Play action: Give each guest a package, and one at a time, they are to deliver it to the person *described* on the wrapping. The description can be written in any mysterious fashion such as a cryptic puzzle, an actual object, or as a poem. For example, for a girl named Penny, pennies could be taped all over the box.

Hints and tips: If the name does not loan itself to decoration, use something the person is famous for, such as: a prize-winning baker's gift could have pictures of pies pasted on it; an avid golfer's box might have golf tees, fake grass, or a photo of a famous golfer on it. For a person who watches soap operas religiously, the package might have soap stars' photos, hearts, and lace or a hanky taped to it.

Name of the game: Halves

Type: Gift-giving.   **# of players:** Any

Supplies: Gift packages; proverbs (two matching halves); hat.

Formation: Players will actively hunt.

Object of the game: Hunting for a present.

Play action: Distribute packages around the room. On each of them should be a sticker with half a proverb on it. The guest will draw the other half of the proverb from a hat, and find the matching gift.

Adaptation: You can substitute any variation of special pairs for the proverb–famous couples, animals and their babies, song titles and singers, etc.

Name of the game: Balloon Bouquet

Type: Gift-giving.   **# of players:** Any

Supplies: Balloons; guest name tags; small papers with a number on them.

Formation: Guests, one at a time, will bust balloons and seek a gift.

Object of the game: Fun way to give gifts.

Play action: Prepare a balloon bouquet especially for gifts. On small pieces of paper, write numbers or symbols corresponding to ones you've written on guests' name tags. Fold and insert one paper slip into each balloon before inflating it. At prize time, ask a guest to select a balloon, sit on it, burst it, and find the paper hidden inside. The guest whose name tag matches the balloon slip wins a prize!

Adaptation: Enclose the numbers inside small boxes and gift wrap. The box must be opened to see who wins a prize.

Adaptation: Make theme-related cupcakes. Draw winner symbols on small pieces of paper for as many door prizes as you have. Before baking, fold the papers (you can put them in tiny foil packages) and slip them into the batter for a selected few. Those who "chew paper" at refreshment time get a prize!

Name of the game: Steal-a-Gift 2

Type: Gift-giving.   **# of players:** Small groups of 5 or 6

Supplies: One deck of cards for each group or table; one gift per person; timer.

Formation: Small group of people around a card table. A stack of small gifts (enough for each player) are in the middle of the table.

Object of the game: To get and keep as many gifts as possible.

Play action: Players are dealt two cards. If they get an ace, they can take one gift from the gift pile. When these gifts are gone, they can go to another table and steal a gift from its pile. If they are dealt either a joker or a king, they must return a gift to the pile if they have one. Try for a ten-minute game.

11.

THE BOLD RELIEF OF LEADERSHIP

I am the most spontaneous speaker in the world because every word, every gesture, and every retort has been carefully rehearsed.
—GEORGE BERNARD SHAW

If you can master good leadership, you will be taking the best first step toward getting your guests relaxed and comfortable. Most people today live harried, busy lives, and they want to put their confidence in something besides themselves, even if only for a few hours at a games party. You want your efforts to *look effortless,* and that absolutely calls for planning ahead.

PLANNING AHEAD
By thinking about important organizational concepts before an event, the key principles will be planted clearly in your mind. The simple steps outlined here are meant to provide reassurance to those who charge ahead and confidence to those who lead with fingers crossed behind their back. But remember, nothing will give you confidence like the experience of doing it.

Novice or not, you still need to make a personal commitment to dive in, to create the great plans you have in mind. If you have to push past predictable feelings of shyness and trepidation, look at it this way: the next time you play leader, it will get easier, faster. Don't let embarrassment or reticence prevent you from doing what you want. Keep the big picture in mind. At least you are out there doing things, and there will be people who appreciate you and the efforts you make, and they will willingly follow. Your friends and loved ones will not only be energized by what it is you want to do but they will cooperate and broadcast that cooperation to others. Some of them will eventually volunteer to help you.

Leading is easy when you make it *appear* easy. Think of the terms "leader" and "host" as synonymous, because in entertaining—no matter what kind of entertaining we are talking about—after organization, motivation, and good food, the other ace for any successful event is leadership. Leadership attitudes, fairness, acceptance, and planning are most of what provides the basis for good hosting and an invigorating and memorable time for all involved.

TAKE ME TO YOUR LEADER

From our earliest memories we recognize that someone has to make assignments, grade papers, and rap knuckles. (Better to avoid knuckle-rapping at our functions!) Still, it's important for the entertainer—and we all act as entertainers in a manner of speaking—to know haw to lift the banner and lead the way.

For those of you who think that leadership is not an integral part of every gathering, big or small, consider what happens at any successful dinner party. As host, you have to get your guests to change from one sequence to the next: to move from introductions through to drinks and conversations and to dinner, through the courses, and into the final phase of relaxing and interacting. And in order to do this, you need leadership strategy and a planned program.

Leadership Qualities

The trick to effective leadership and hosting is to find your unique combination of assertiveness, coupled with pleasant speech and a planned, polished presentation—in order to get people to do what you want.

We've all, at one time or another, attended a party where we've been subjected to a commandant type of leader barking commands. Oh, it's true, things get done—and there will always be those who jump to please—but the end result is not very pleasant. Too much direction from a militant host seems uncaring and rude and, consequently, people are turned off and soon cease to cooperate.

On the other hand, a request presented *indirectly* will probably get ignored. Nothing will happen, because the leader did not make his/her wishes clear. A leader who expects that guests will know intuitively what is being asked is going to be sorely disappointed unless, of course, the guests are all psychics.

There's another methodology, too—that of the "controlling" type leader. And, truthfully, no one I've ever met has enjoyed being manipulated by a control freak. She's the one who operates as if you were a child, talking you through everything, usually in a condescending manner. This discourages any form of freedom or creativeness—no time for that!

These are not the kinds of leaders we care to emulate. And I'm sure it comes as no surprise that we're not all born with a gene for leadership, even though some of us would like to think we have a corner on that particular DNA. So, let's look at this squarely: it is not easy to lead and be effective. How do we proceed?

Star in Your Own Mental Video

First of all, you need to plan ahead. I hear you saying to yourself, "If I script everything out, there won't be any fun or spontaneity." But this isn't necessarily the case. Planning or visualizing what it is you want to have happen—mentally seeing yourself delivering instructions or delegating work to others—will help set a much-needed foundation of confidence and will act as an aid in building up your poise. With a smooth program of events outlined in your head, you will have a better sense of direction, because you've anticipated all the glitches, and your *knowing* will help to put others at ease.

Much of leadership has to do with "herding"—getting small, or even large, groups of people either to perform a task or to move. You'll soon realize you do not want to be responsible for moving eight—or eighty—people in one direction, and find you have to move them the other way or cancel the whole thing out. That's a lot of people-energy at your command—too much to waste! Better to harness that energy, and get it right the first time!

So make the initial effort to think out the whole evening or event and run it through your mind like a film. Professional speechmakers and seminar leaders not only know their lines—but they will tell you that this scripting technique helps them master the event. And in the case of leaders who actively pursue physical goals with others, like coaches and theater directors, logistical imaging is timely and prevents movements chaos.

From now on, make it a point when you are working:
- to keep notes in your party journal about how the games worked.
- to include a reminder to "visualize."
- to allot a chunk of time for mental leadership practice.

Twenty minutes of quiet time ought to do it. Close your eyes; picture the event beginning—greeting guests, hanging up coats, etc.—and then think about your role in facilitating the event, through every activity, all the way to the time when you see yourself bidding good-bye and closing the door on a great night!

Taking Charge

Since your leadership position *begins at the door* upon your guests' arrival at the beginning of gathering, a meeting, or in the reception line at a big event, use this subtle form of dominion to establish yourself right away. It gives people a "first contact" individual. It says, in a guest's mind, "Hey, this person is in charge." Even when I am putting on a simple get-together, I never let anyone take away my shot at greeting participants. It's my first opportunity to gain control.

As people arrive, go to the foyer and open the door with a smile and a nice "Hi." Usher them in with a shake of their hand, hugs for those more familiar, or a gentle touch on the arm. This kind of demonstration says, "Hello, you're welcome," in more ways than the obvious one. Surveys have proven that body language is never wasted. People are smart enough, and children are savvy enough, to recognize whether they are wanted or not. They will pick up on any mixed signals that manage to get through.

All generations may say it, but this is a different time we live in. Trying to get ten people to agree on anything is a real challenge. Everyone has an opinion, and many have clearly demonstrated needs. In addition, people have a host of outside commitments. They are involved with sports and hobby clubs, community causes, and functions, or maybe they are traveling for their jobs; they get hit up for alumni/ae concerns, as board members, on neighborhood watches, in their children's schools, in churches and synagogues, in work for non-profits—and the list goes on. To put it into perspective then, everybody is busy with their lives and *you called this meeting*, so lighten up! Really demonstrate your "people sense," and then, enjoy what it is you want to do.

Take a few extra, deliberate moments to get guests in the door. Allow them to get acclimated, hang up their coats, chat about inclement weather and other "making nice" topics, and then move them to an area of comfort for an icebreaking activity they can glom onto—a small chore, an introduction to a mutual friend, a guided tour, something of interest. Pairing an individual with a partner and sending them off on a hunt can be an excellent choice for new arrivals.

If the weather has indeed been inclement, have a bench or a settee where guests can remove boots, pull off hats, scarves, etc., and set aside a place for their belongings. A closet is preferable, but you could use a special coat rack or even pegs on the wall. Make room ahead of time. No one wants to feel than their seasonal-weather accoutrements are making a mess on the carpet or clogging up a hallway.

Forget the Lampshade

Sometime during the party or event you will need the spotlight, perhaps even a microphone, the podium, or a blackboard. Position is an all-important factor for getting attention. Being seen and heard is the mainstay of all good leader presentations and you need to be in a prominent position in order to get noticed.

Sometimes the *odd* vantage point provides a distinct advantage. For example, once I was in charge of an extremely large party with seventy people, half of whom were teenagers, and we were at an outside location—a lakeside pavilion. Although the picnic tables were situated under a large roofed-in enclosure, I was competing for attention with boaters, bird song, and other picnickers. To compensate for the open-air acoustics, I climbed up on a bench at the head of the pavilion in order to make announcements and give instructions.

Nothing is more frustrating for guests than not to hear the speaker. So if you first raise one or both arms as a signal, that will serve to quiet people down. If you are outdoors or in a large auditorium, a sound signal (use a whistle only if outdoors) or a chord played on an instrument would be appropriate. Often there will be individuals within the group who react to this quickly and help you by cueing in the others. You might follow up on this action by calling out,

"May I have your attention please?" but usually if you are simply patient and wait for the room to settle, it will come together without further intervention.

If you jump the gun without waiting for quiet, people will not hear you and they'll turn to each other and ask, "What did she say?" or "Did you hear that?"—and the whispering will prevent them from giving you their full attention. If you have a problem waiting for quiet due to nervousness, count to at least twenty in your head before speaking.

We Hear You

Once at center stage, be concise. You have a specific purpose and it is best not to try to hold your guests to attention too long. Some people have only moments of attention to give. All you need do is make a brief introduction, give announcements, provide instructions, or bring about a change in activity.

Leaders who deliver long-winded dissertations lose the hard-won motivation of their guests. And should the leaders/speakers be ill-prepared, inarticulate, or concerned with drawing attention to themselves, they will lose the respect of the audience before they can say "Ho-hum." A group responds favorably to clear directions given in a friendly, pleasant manner accompanied by a smile. A minimum of distraction, delay, repetition, and confusion can make the difference between genuine enjoyment and forced participation.

Also remember, in situations where the dynamics are grand and the number of participants great, even a mispronunciation gives an audience pause. Use well-thought-out words and short, direct sentences in order to maintain enthusiasm and propel the audience into the next action.

Ready, Set—Go!

If, as part of your entertaining plan, you decide to play a series of games—there are other things you need to know in order to lead. This section will provide some tips on transitions, timing, and formations.

One probable, very obvious rule of leading games is that leaders almost never take part in the games themselves. I view this as a small enough sacrifice, because I generally enjoy starting, stimulating, and monitoring the play more than anything. The leader has a unique opportunity—to watch people having fun. And as the players lose their inhibitions and try new things, a real sense of human interaction and connection takes place among those involved. I am not trying to make this sound like a religious experience, but it is very moving and can be extremely rewarding to conduct a great games party.

Shift Left, Drop Back, Pitch Right . . .

The goal of any good planned games event is to create a relaxed atmosphere for guests so that one activity flows into the next with-

out rush or disorder. This takes considerable planning. Much like a coach who directs the plays for his team, the host of a games party also has a game plan.

I'm sure at one time or another we've all been the unfortunate pawn of a leader who is confused, who repeatedly attempts to get attention, and who—through rearrangement of furniture or people—produces either tension or boredom for the participants. This won't be you!

First, ahead of time, write out the games you want to play. Print them out on index cards. Games, as you've seen in this book, are usually broken down into distinct categories that identify their purpose: icebreakers, defrosters or get-acquainted games, contests or pre-party games, team relay or action games, pencil-and-paper or quiet table games, music games and hunts, or special-events games. Planning ahead will ensure that transitions within a game or between games are carried out harmoniously. For example, you wouldn't open with a team relay if players didn't know each other, and you probably wouldn't ask game players to do a hunt after late-night eating (they won't want to go out!). So, first of all, think about the pace you want for the evening, who the people are, how much time you have, and what your facilities are like.

If your guests are not acquainted, it makes sense to start out with a game that introduces them to each other. Look for games that require people to interact in order to achieve a goal, something that forces them to move around and either speak to or examine others at play.

Okay, Time to Punt—

After you deliver the instruction for your game, establish a signal for starting and stopping so the group is aware of your parameters. That way, they will listen for the beginning signal, and even though in their exuberance they may keep playing when it's time to stop, they will recognize the signal for terminating the activity. For instance, you may say, "This game is called 'Mystery Guest.' You all circulate around the room and try to find out as much as possible about each guest, making notes as you go. Keep this data with you. At the end of the party, I will read a list of facts about the mystery guest. As soon as you recognize who that person is, shout out their name. If you are right you will win a prize."

You might have the room set up ahead of time with as few physical obstacles as possible, to facilitate people's roaming around. After about ten minutes allowed for this activity, you might want to move guests into a circle formation, or toward a second mixer. If you follow that with a sit-down or table game, that signals guests toward another transition and settles them in for food and quiet chatter. They will know each other better by then, so the meal atmosphere will be less strained and conversation should be brisk. See how this works? Now, this is just one example of the many hundreds of variations and types of moods and activities that can be constructed with some positive planning.

TIMING

Like a juggler, the best party leader knows that timing is the difference between a clean catch and a rude thump on the head. With experience you will gain more confidence, and be better able to judge what constitutes good balance for how long an activity should take, and how to move from one game adventure into setting the stage for the next.

Here are a few techniques to achieve game harmony:
- Distribute materials if necessary.
- Give directions and establish your signals for start and stop.
- Ask for questions, then begin.
- After the first game ends, give results or a prize.
- Move right along, giving formation instructions for the next game.
- Ask for questions.
- Provide new signals, continue, and so on.

You will be using descriptive rules and precise terminology so your guests will not be left out in the cold. Before giving directions for an activity, it is wise to have the group in the desired formation and all materials available or in the hands of the players. Explanations to participants are made more simple by using a phrase such as "Will the six lucky winners come to the front. . ." and then, after rewarding them, spacing them out in front of the room and saying, "Now all the rest of you form lines of five behind them." Smooth, rhythmic, and choreographed to flow, movements like this mean your guests and players will have a ball with the least amount of frustration.

Whoa, Nellie!
Knowing when to stop is not only important, it is a leader's primary responsibility. Sometimes a game provides an easy out–all action stops when the game score is reached, players are eliminated, the music ceases, or a particular team finishes first. It's the other games you need watch out for. Careful observation will usually cue you in to when stimulation has reached its peak for the greatest number of players. At this point you can call, "Time," "Stop," "Hold it," or "Okay, attention." And, then, wait for them to stop before you begin talking again, because your players will still be keyed up and you don't want to run over their fun. Of course, the exact time to quit an activity is hard to determine, but, psychologically, I always think of it as the point at which people are still having a good time and want more.

For those trickier timing sequences, here is a list with some other tangible signs:

1. Self-directed contests are some of the best ways to keep guests engrossed while they are waiting for the others. With a cardboard sign giving directions, no monitoring is needed. (Just remember to announce the correct answer and award prizes for the closest guess, nearest amount, exact count, etc.)

2. Since pre-party games give those waiting something to do while others are still arriving, allow about ten to fifteen minutes for them.

3. Mixers and get-acquainted games usually stay good for about 5 to 10 minutes. Your instincts will tell you if this is working.

4. Sometimes it is your call to set a definite time to stop an activity, or to determine a score to end play. Practice the game ahead of time with your family and use a timer. Write down what you find out.

5. Puzzles and tricks will keep people interested in guessing, or looking for a solution, through five to eight repeated attempts.

6. A noisy active game, or relay, will keep players involved for a fairly substantial length of time. Count on about ten minutes, but be aware that it may become tiresome for some (age is a factor).

7. Skits or presentations should take no more than five minutes. Shoot for three as an average.

Every Batman Has a Robin

A good assistant is a treasure (and don't let him/her forget it). A second person can be invaluable for distributing and collecting supplies, keeping track of the timer or clock, coordinating supplies, retrieving gifts, playing music, demonstrating specific moves, and getting people into formations. Your assistant will spring into action when you say, "Let's hold hands and form a circle here." If you pick someone who follows directions well, and has the shine of enthusiasm and a cooperative nature, your job will be so much more pleasant. Go over the program in advance with your assistant(s), doing a walk-through, a demonstration, if necessary, or presenting notes on how to carry out specific duties. Use as many helpers as you need.

The Steps Required for Good Host Leadership
1. **Decide what your mission is.**
   Determine ahead of time what it is you want to accomplish or have happen.

2. **Write a plan.**
   Sit down with pencil and paper and devise a leadership plan.
   Plot out what needs to happen and how best to accomplish it.
3. **Visualize**
   Picture the event in your mind from beginning to end, outlin-
   ing your role in that production.
4. **Introductions**
   Use this tool to establish yourself as leader and to set a mood
   of cooperation and enthusiasm.
5. **Position**
   Arrange to be in a spot where people can both see and hear
   you. It keeps guests from becoming frustrated or bored.
6. **Attention**
   Develop what you think will be the best ways to gain and
   keep an audience's attention. Your two best tools are visibility
   and sound signals.

7. **Waiting**

Learn to be patient and wait for attention and quiet. It could mean the death of your program if you don't.

8. **Instructions**

Familiarize yourself and your assistants with the directions. This homework will pay off when you're getting people involved and moving in an orderly and focused way.

9. **Watch**

Be observant of the behavior cues of your guests. Make a mental note of the overall mood. Seek a good balance between tension and stimulation, relaxation and fun.

10. **Transitions**

Learn how to create smooth and flowing sequences with some careful planning and notes.

11. **Timing**

The factor all leaders are most concerned about—timing—is your chief concern, too.

12. **Assistants**

Make good use of assistants and treat them well; they will prove invaluable.

THE FUNCTION OF INTRODUCTION

If you think about making introductions as a way of giving presents, you're halfway there. You are, in simple terms, "presenting" one acquaintance or friend to another. For example, you would say, "Colonel Mustard, may I present my husband, Michael Campbell. Michael, this is Colonel Mustard." If you feel the terminology of *presenting* is too formal or unnatural for you, simply say, "Miss Scarlet, this is my son Jordan Campbell. Jordan, this is Miss Scarlet, an important character in both books and games."

The only real rule to remember in the function of introduction is that you present a younger person to an older one, a person of no rank to someone who does have rank, such as an honored judge, a military officer, or a senator. And, you would also present a peer to an out-of-town visitor. "David, may I present my good friend, Jill Aubry. Jill, this is Mr. David Rainey, my boss at the Arkansas School for Mathematics and Sciences." For peer-to-peer introductions, it doesn't matter who is introduced to whom, although I generally prefer to present men to women. And remember to use both first and last names.

By the way, one thing you might consider when making introductions: It's not a bad idea to provide name tags for new acquaintances. Any extra information you can supply will enable the newly acquainted to launch into conversation, which I think is the point of the introduction to begin with.

More Tips about Host Leadership:

1. Wear your most put-together comfortable clothes. A twisted seam, straining buttons, or a ripped hem can prevent you from giving your all. Don't let your "look" divert attention from your message. Many experts confirm that if you dress neatly, your good appearance makes others feel more trustful and more generous toward you than if you dress down.
2. Don't apologize. We have all experienced being invited to someone's home and having the hostess apologize for one thing after the other. Either you are ready or not, and excuses will not convince others of your efficiency.
3. Check all equipment, supplies, and game pieces early on.
4. Don't be shifty mentally or physically. Shifting your weight from foot to foot gives the impression you haven't committed yourself and it looks immature.
5. Understand what motivates people and try to provide it.
6. Nervous? Consider joining the Toastmaster's International in your region. This group is the world's largest organization devoted to training individuals in public speaking, communication, and leadership skills.
7. Use note cards for reminders if your memory is go-i-n . . .

12.
GAFFS, "UH-OHS," AND HOW TO SOLVE THEM

Grace under pressure. —ERNEST HEMINGWAY

I can't believe that Murphy had a law for everything. But unless you've been living in a cave, you have to admit that when you're planning an event, anything can go wrong. In this chapter we'll look at what happens when reality cramps the style of imagination. The first overall suggestion pertaining to a party dilemma is to analyze it as if it were happening to someone else. In other words, don't get emotionally upset. A clear head and quick, decisive action is the best way to go.

TROUBLE, TROUBLE

Drunkenness
Here are some sly but surefire tips to avoid situations with alcohol abuse:
- Make a drinker's choice weaker than usual
- Measure drinks more precisely using a jigger, and pour into smaller glasses
- Keep the cocktail hour to *an hour*
- Prepare plenty of finger foods, hors d'oeuvres
- Make fantastic nonalcoholic alternatives available
- Have punchbowl substitutes
- Give guests things to do while waiting for more substantial foods
- Schedule an extended dessert and coffee period
- If necessary, refuse them another and put bottles away; say you are moving to another phase of the party
- Use the designated driver rule, or call for cab service
- Let them sleep it off in your guest room

Remember, in some places the host can be held legally accountable if a drunken guest kills someone in a car accident.

Illness

If someone in your immediate family has come down with the flu or any other communicable illness, either move the party to another location, substitute a dinner out (on your tab), or reschedule.

Belligerence

Say guests begin arguing and it looks as though things might escalate. You have no choice but to quickly and calmly get these guests to leave. It is not up to you to apply a patch, or to allow the offenders time to work it out. Promptly, after they have left, turn up the music, or present another event or surprise.

One guest seems to be sniping at another, and is acting publicly rude

Your responsibility to your guests dictates that you break up this behavior quickly. Suggest to the offender that his comments are not to your liking and that perhaps he would prefer to leave. Resume your events without any discourse and rechannel the direction so guests feel comfortable and are quickly engaged in something else.

Guest puts out a cigarette on the floor

Simple. Do not allow smoking in your house. A designated "smoking area" complete with sand-filled bowls or receptacles on a deck or in a discreet driveway area with chairs will suffice.

A featured dish gets ruined

Substitute something else on a fine plate, and in the future, make no-fuss dishes or treats. If you are low on provisions, call for take-out, but serve it on attractive ceramic or glass dishware—no paper containers or cartons.

You smell marijuana or find someone using or distributing drugs

Be firm and insist that this guest leave, with the words, "This is against the law and it will not happen in my house." Usher them out a back or side door as soon as possible, and make no excuse for their absence.

You find out a guest has charged many expensive long-distance calls to your number

Your problem here is with the telephone company. Call the business office of your provider and explain that the calls were made without your knowledge or consent. Let them handle the follow-up and collection.

Guests arrive late

Don't assume they are arriving late to annoy you. Invite them into your home graciously and get them acclimated as quickly as possible. You may want one of your assistants to bring them up to speed without disturbing the progress of the others. If they show up in the middle of a game, suggest they may want to help out as a photographer. Give them a camera and let them at it.

If the event is a dinner party:

How long do you wait? Professional dinner-givers have their own personal guidelines of course, but for most, here is an example:

If your dinner invitation was for 7:30 p.m. and you had planned to serve the meal within an hour:

- It's generally a good idea to allow 30–45 minutes for the cocktail activities.
- If the no-shows have not arrived by 8:30 p.m., you might want to give them a phone call to see if they've left (or forgotten), and a message left on their answering machine for their concern is only right.
- Open the dinner wine to breathe, light the candles, and place the cold soup or salad on the table.
- Moments before the designated serving time, remove their place settings with the most efficient aplomb you can master. Pour the wine after guests are seated.

If the guests do show up late, don't reprimand them or ask questions. Late guests may have had any number of misfortunes, and you need to rise above rude behavior and continue to shine as the gracious and friendly person you are. Reset their place settings with a minimum of fuss, pushing back any feelings about abuse, or deliberateness. Give them the benefit of the doubt, when possible.

For habitual no-show offenders or people who continually cancel without explanation or apology, it's up to you where to draw the line. No one can give you a definite rule except to suggest that you assess them on a case-by-case basis. In the future when you reach those people's names, you may decide to remove them from the guest list and avoid any chance of failure. If they have legitimate explanations you may offer hospitality again, but if they are tight-lipped or obviously stalling, you might reluctantly remove them as guests.

The electricity goes out

You were prepared and have ready a series of oil lamps, candles, flashlights, and other means of illumination. You can always play a quiet talking game until service is returned. You might even use the ambiance to create a game out of spooky storytelling.

A nonplayer refuses to join in the action

Do not coerce your guests, but suggest that he/she may want to aid you in some way, for example by keeping score, readying supplies for the next game, acting as official timer, handing out game equipment, photographing the event, or simply acting as the audience.

If your task is to highlight an unusual event, what kind of setting is different?

Hold the party in a museum, a gallery, on a boat, in a park, at the base of a mountain, in an airplane hanger, in a decorator house—but try to match the theme and games with the place.

A pet is misbehaving, barking, or disturbing a guest

If your pet is not mature, or acclimated to company and events, board the little dear at a kennel or hire someone to take him into their home to "dog-sit." Understand that not everyone loves animals and a guest may even have allergies, an aversion to pets, or a fear of Fido.

Cautions and Safety

Pay particular attention to traffic patterns, to tight spaces, narrow pathways or irregular cobblestones, traffic-heavy corridors, or over-

worked bathrooms—ouch! These are things that you need to think about ahead of time, not only for your guests' welfare but sometimes for your own sanity.

Parking

If your community has an ordinance about street parking, you should know about it before your guests present you with their tickets. You may want to talk with your neighbors about using their driveways.

Electrical and Other illumination

Often extra illumination or equipment is needed. Make sure to check outlets to see if they are overloaded. Have your assistant monitor candles or any objects with an open flame. Keep an extinguisher handy around gas and fire grills, or in areas where oil or fat is frying. If electrical cords must cross a pathway, take the time to tape over the cable with duct tape so guests won't trip or become trapped. Check for crossed, broken, or stretched wires.

Hazards in General

A mention of items to look out for: flammable objects, hanging objects, pointed articles, sharp corners, hot pots and spots, precariously perched artifacts and other dangerous props, water hazards, wet areas, etc.

Getting There

Provide written instructions along with your maps. Why not attach a photo of your house? Mark your territory well—I can't tell you how many guests get lost! Nothing is more frustrating for your friends than circling the block like a vulture, trying to find a party. Take into account other considerations like having your house numbers lit at night, advising guests about streets that circle back onto themselves or that involve intersections in incomprehensible ways. In difficult cases, it might be worth your while to designate an area or landmark where guests can meet and them follow your assistant the rest of the way.

WEATHER

Wasn't it Mark Twain who said, "Everyone talks about the weather but nobody does anything about it"? You might not be able to affect the weather you get, but you can do something about it. Make advance plans. Have advice ready for guests in the event of rain, snow, etc., and know when to just call off the party.

13.

THE INTERSECTION BETWEEN "OVER" AND "DO IT AGAIN"

Hear no evil—speak no evil—and you'll never be invited to a party.
—OSCAR WILDE

The party's over and you're basking in the glow of comments such as: "I had so much fun on Saturday, I can't tell you how funny it was when . . ." "Harold said to tell you that the hunt was the best time he's had in years." "Why don't you come over for dominoes next Tuesday; we want to thank you for the party."

Drink it all in. You deserve it. It's not too many people nowadays that go out of their way to offer others the magic of interaction. It's a heady feeling to have bridged the barrier most people live behind. Why, it's better than sliced bread! Not to mention the lasting effects of a successful party, which are more memorable than those of almost any other form of entertainment.

PARTY JOURNAL

While you're in this mood, make some notes in your party journal. Write down what you feel were the key things that worked for you and your guests, such as "Guests really liked the creative aspects of designing a gift hat at the shower," "Remember that Tom is allergic to milk products," "The hunt in the great room ran about fifteen minutes." That way, the next time you think about a game-playing party again, you will remember the dos, the don'ts, and how to really personalize events to make them better.

Run the party back over in your mind, step by step, and make notes about things that will help you in the future. Perhaps you will decide to pep up the style—"Guests were exhilarated when we played the competitive games"—or slow it down by using more pencil-and-paper games for your intellectual crew.

Write down who sat next to whom; perhaps a couple who laughed and danced will make great partners at the next party. Which combinations of people worked, and which ones didn't? Who came in late? You may want to invite them to come ten minutes early the next time. These are all important thoughts. Log them in your journal.

You may also decide to start a file of ideas, games, and recipes you want to try. Keep them with your journal. Make a note of foods that people are partial to and also ones that they can't eat for either dietary or religious reasons. Orthodox Jews do not eat pork or shellfish. Muslims will not eat these foods and also will not partake of alcohol of any kind. Hindus will eat no beef, and strict Catholics prefer not to eat meat during Lent. These religions not only prohibit certain foods, but their followers are not even supposed to be in close proximity to them. Worth noting.

This is also a good place to keep business cards from caterers, rental agencies, and party stores.

PARTY CLOSET

If you designate an area in a closet for party supplies, it will be easier to throw an event at any time, even at the last minute. Perhaps during the year you can collect party napkins, coordinating plates, and partyware with designs you particularly like.

This also is a good place to store candles, votives, and candlesticks. You may want to order them by the box, and keep them lying flat, in a cool place. Also collect wooden matches (and never throw out the empty boxes—they're used in games!) Sterno cans, lanterns, and luminarias.

You might also house your sterling, flatware, or special serving pieces all together in one central spot. Don't forget to include floral supplies in a basket along with your party supplies. Tuck scissors, ribbon, wire, and floral foam along with smooth rocks, stickum, and frogs (the green metal spikes placed in the bottom of containers to keep flowers from falling over or crushing other stems), or those little vial containers big enough for a single bud.

I buy party gifts and favors all year long. Napkin rings, attractive boxes, scented bath essentials, figurines, small pieces of art, craft items, anything that strikes my fancy during the year that I think would make a nice surprise or a surefire prize. Keep your eyes open and collect posters, flags, and pennants—you can always find a way to use them. This area of your closet might be the best place to store your wrapping supplies as well. Gift-wrap materials—like ribbon, foils, markers, and tape, along with card stock, special pens, and place cards—can all wait here together, ready for your next event.

This party area of your closet can accommodate the more unusual items that add a festive touch to a party but that are seldom used. Store fresh bags of sand, candle stubs, plate warmers and hot trays, extension cords, soft and decorative lightbulbs, party lanterns, fondue pots, and the odd utensils. Add dress-up clothes, costumes, hats, clown makeup, and wardrobe artifacts. You will be ready for anything.

This may be a good place to keep larger items, athletic supplies, or the objects you use to build an obstacle course or set up a relay. Stock a soccer ball, tennis rackets and balls, Frisbees, hula hoops, beach balls, and various other outdoor equipment here.

If you cannot afford to give over a closet or any part of it, you can group your entertaining supplies in a large hamper, a special box, or a chest of drawers. The idea is to have everything at the ready and eliminate the pressure of collecting all the pieces. Remember—when you shop antique stores, discount houses, dime stores, specialty shops, or garage sales—keep your party closet in mind. That way, when you travel around you will automatically spot special invitations, napkins, or that particular mug for a gift that will enhance your next big event.

Keep a list of what you have stored, something to help you remember the right "have on hand" items that are so important when entertaining. Perhaps you will want to keep salt and pepper pairs, candy dishes, coffee pots, wine carafes, stainless serving bins, brandy snifters, champagne flutes, trivets, tooth and party picks, fishware, corn cob holders, mirrors, nut picks . . . well, you get the idea.

Like the spotlights going out at the end of the play, we've reached the end of this book. You have all the tools at hand for your "performance." I've given you everything you need to create a fun, interactive event, and now the magic is up to you. So, stuff the rabbit back into the hat and ready the stage for your act—I have the feeling it will be one great show!

APPENDICES A–G

APPENDIX A.   BIRTHDAY CONSIDERATIONS

For special birthday considerations, it helps to have some knowledge of the person's birthstone and the flower associated with his or her special month. Set the color theme to coordinate with that particular gem and flower.

Look for special cards that document the significant events that happened in the year of their birth that tell what the cost of living was, the most popular music, movie, or fashion, etc. What a nice way to look back in time to the importance of one's arrival.

MONTH	BIRTHSTONE	FLOWER
January	Garnet	Carnation or Snowdrop
February	Amethyst	Violet or Primrose
March	Aquamarine	Jonquil
April	Diamond	Sweet Pea or Daisy
May	Emerald	Lily of the Valley or Hawthorn
June	Pearl or Moonstone	Rose or Honeysuckle
July	Ruby	Larkspur or Water Lily
August	Sardonyx or Peridot	Poppy or Gladiolus
September	Sapphire	Aster or Morning Glory
October	Opal or Tourmaline	Calendula or Cosmos
November	Topaz	Chrysanthemum
December	Turquoise or Lapis Lazuli	Narcissus or Holly

APPENDIX B.
CLEANING AND DÉCOR CHECKLIST

After the first four years, the dirt doesn't get any worse.

—QUENTIN CRISP

Clean Barbecue Grill
Clean Bath(s)
Clean Bedrooms
Clean Coffee Urn
Clean Cooler for Beverages/Ice
Clean Den
Clean Dining Room
Clean Family Room
Clean Foyer
Clean Garage
Clean Guest Room
Clean Kitchen
Clean Living Area
Clean Oven (Microwave)
Clean Patio/Deck/Terrace
Clean Pool
Clean Refrigerator
Clean Shower Curtain/Liner
Clean Stairway
Clean Space in Coat Closet
Defrost Freezer
Last Dish Washing/Put Away
Last Kitchen Cleaning
Last-Minute Cleaning Touch-Ups
Laundry
Polish Silver/Brass/Copper
Touch Up Bath(s)
Wash Bath Rugs/Carpets
Wash Bath Towels
Wash Ceiling Light Fixtures/Fans
Wash Chandelier(s)
Wash China in Cabinet
Wash Crystal/Glassware
Wash Dishes/Run Dishwasher
Wash Kitchen Cabinets
Wash Serving Pieces/Utensils

Wash Windows
Wash/Fill Salt and Peppers
Yard Cleanup
Garage Sweep
Outdoor Lighting Check
Extra Seating/ Tables
Check All Lightbulbs
Decorate House
Decorate Outside
Put Away Personal Belongings
Put Away Treasures
Put Decorative Towels in Baths
Put Soaps/Tissues in Baths
Repot/Move/Clean Up Plants
Set Décor Lighting/Dimmers
Set Table/Buffet
Set Up Music/ Entertainment
Test Indoor/Outdoor/Special Lighting
Turn On Music
Decorate Christmas Tree
Decorate Garland/Wreaths

APPENDIX C.
ESTIMATING COSTS

As in any plan, there are a variety of items to think about when preparing a budget. Following are some notes about expense extras.

- Plan for valet-type parking attendants (college students can always use the extra money).
- Factor in lawn and other maintenance services so people will have a cleared and unencumbered path into your event.
- Prepare enough food for at least two invisible guests for small events but, for larger affairs, an extra two servings for every ten people ought to suffice.
- An additional dessert item.
- Rentals of coffee urns, extremely large serving pieces or warmers.
- Funds for new linen or décor items.
- Balloon bouquets, signs, or easels posted as markers leading toward the event are helpful, plus they help to establish a certain party spirit.
- Have extra cash available for unexpected runs for ice, etc.
- In additional to outdoor lighting, think about using luminaria during the holiday season, torchieres in the summer, citronella if on the patio or deck, or string-hanging plastic party lamps for more casual parties.

And—know your financial plans and parameters ahead of time.

There is an amusing advertisement for a credit card company in which the bride's father is beaming at his daughter while she dances with the groom; then the camera cuts to the father receiving the catering bill with an additional $200 allotted for parsley. Finally, the camera cuts again one last time to the exiting couple and pans over to their limousine driver with his hand out, into which the bride's father relinquishes his credit card. Not so farfetched. Knowing what services are covered, even down to being prepared for tipping, are cautions that should not go unheeded unless you are extremely calm in heart and deep of pocket.

APPENDIX D.

PARTY PLAN TEMPLATE:

Type: _____

Purpose: _____

No. of Guests: : _____

Honored Guests: _____

Where: _____

Date: _____

Time: _____

Invitation: _____

Food: _____

_____

Décor: _____

_____

Games/Activities: _____

_____

Gifts, Favors, Prizes: _____

_____

Special Considerations: _____

_____

_____

_____

_____

APPENDIX F. TYPE OF PARTIES AND VARIOUS OCCASIONS FROM A TO Z

A—
All-night Graduation Party
Alumni/ae Gathering
Anniversary
April Fool's Day
Auction Event

B—
Baby Shower
Bachelor Party
Baptism
Bar Mitzvah/Bat Mitzvah
Barbecue
Bastille Day
Beach Party
Birthday
　Adult
　Child
　Twenty-First
　Fortieth
　Sixtieth
　Seventy-Fifth
　Hundredth
Block Party
Book Discussion
Bon Voyage
Bowling Meet
Bridal Shower
Bridal Tea
Bride's Dinner
Bridesmaid's Dinner
Bridge Party
Brunch
Buffet
Bunko
Business Associate Dinner

C—
Casino Party
Cast Party (Theater Group)

Children's Party
Chinese New Year's
Christening
Christmas Caroling
Christmas Day Dinner
Christmas Eve Dinner
Christmas Open House
Christmas Party (with Piñata
　and Santa Claus)
Cinco de Mayo
Clam Bake
Class Reunion
Club Brunch
Cocktail Party
Coffee Party
College Crew Party
Columbus Day
Coming Out
Commemoration Fetes
Confirmation
Convocation
Cookie Exchange Party
Couple's Shower
Crafter's Club

D—
Dancing
Demonstration
Derby Day Party
Dessert Party
Dinner, Sit Down
Dinner, Specialty (Ethnic)

E—
Earth Day
Easter Dinner
Easter Egg Hunt
Elderly Function
Engagement Party

F—
Family Reunion
Fantasy Football (Baseball)
   Draft
Fashion Show
Father's Day Party
Fiftieth Wedding Anniversary
First Communion
Fund-raising

G—
Games Party
Garage Sale
Good Friday
Graduation Party
   High School
   College
Groom's Dinner

H—
Halloween Party
Hanukkah
Hayride
Housewarming

I—
Ice Cream Social
Ice Skating Meet

J—
July 4th

K—
Kennel Club Meet or Seminar
Kwanza

L—
Labor Day Party
Lakeside Outings
Legislative Announcements
Life Changes
   Going Away
Luncheon

M—
Mardi Gras Party
Martin Luther King Day
Memorial Day
Memorials
Mother-Daughter Luncheon
Mother's Day Celebration
Movie Viewing and Review
Moving In Day Helpout
Mystery Guest
Mystery Party

N—
Neighborhood Block Party
Newcomer Introduction
New Home
New Job Celebration
New Neighbor Welcome
New Year's Day
New Year's Eve Party
Non-occasion Gathering

O—
Once in a Blue Moon
Open House
Overnight Guest

P—
Palm Sunday
Passover
Pet Parade
Picnic
Pinochle Group Plans
Pizza Party (Top-Your-Own)
Pool Party
Potluck Dinner
Presidents' Day

R—
Reception
Religious Holiday
Retirement Party
Reunions

Rosh Hashanah
Rush Party

S—
Salon
Save-the-___ Event
Scavenger Hunt
Shogum Event
Skateland
Slumber Party
Special Occasion
Sporting Event
St. Patrick's Day
Super Bowl Get-Together
Sweet Sixteen Party
Symphony Support

T—
Tailgate Party
Tea
Teenager's Party
Thanksgiving Dinner
The "Big Game" Party
Theme Party (e.g., Barn
    Dance)

Trim the Tree Party
TV Special Party

V—
Valentine's Day Party
Veteran's Day

W—
Wedding
    Bachelor
    Bachelorette
    Gift Opening
Wedding Brunch
Wedding Reception
Wedding Rehearsal Dinner
Welcome Tables
Wine and Cheese Party

Y—
Yom Kippur
Youth Parties

Z—
Zoo Day

APPENDIX G.
PARTY LIFESTYLE PLANNER

0–8 YEARS OLD

These party participants are too young to have much say about what kinds of entertaining are appropriate. Youngsters still have to rely on the patience and goodwill of their elders. The best occasions for this tender age group are birthday celebrations, theme parties (pirates, cowboys, astronauts, and the like), Halloween carnivals, holiday gatherings, Disney viewings, overnight friends, backyard Olympics; contests, relays, game parties and simple hunts, crafting events, cookouts, outings to museums and child-oriented cultural spots; professional entertainments like clowns, magic, or music; simple cooking or baking demonstrations, and anything else that involves adult supervision.

8–16 YEARS OLD

Most of the same types of functions listed above for the 0–8-year-old group still apply, but now the lifestyle is more group-oriented and the attention span is longer. In addition to those activities listed above, for 8–16 you can add in barbecues, pizza parties, Sweet Sixteen, debuts, Bar/Bat Mitzvahs, confirmations, picnics, more outings like skating, bowling, and mall visits; cards and board games hold more fascination as entertainment; dancing, slumber parties, pre-ballgame events, scouting and explorer functions, camping, and more outdoor activities.

16–21 YEARS OLD

The 0–8-year-old activities are loathsome to these ages now, although the middle-adolescent functions are okay, provided adult supervision is cut to a minimum or nonexistent. Add in more glamorous events like proms, graduation and all-night events, college salons, rush parties, dances, room squeezes, and engagement parties.

21–35 YEARS OLD

Education and traveling have probably taken precedence in the life of someone 21–35, but now entertaining can be group-oriented once again, or the occasional romantic dinner. If the individual is now part of a couple, their friendships are paramount until children arrive on the scene. Look forward to adding in events that involve more liquor or food, like cocktail parties or small soirees, club nightlife, and music, or concerts. Fashionable events to see and be seen at are fun for this age group, and community service offers opportunities for games, interaction, and a chance to practice social skills.

35–40 YEARS OLD

If children are around, the need for supervision of many of the events listed for the group 0–14 is of prime consideration. Anything with family takes on new meaning. Add in activities like christenings, receptions, TV parties, and movie evenings; tailgate parties, the Super Bowl, trail rides, bonfires, hosting school events, anniversaries, Thanksgiving and family Christmas dinners, causes and duty-minded events, church group and youth parties, celebrations and caroling, dessert parties, and brunches. Barbecues are more popular than ever, as are shared kitchen cooking evenings and potlucks, wine and cheese get-togethers, New Year's Eve bashes, and milestone festivities.

40–55 YEARS OLD

At-home functions take precedence, and these ages are probably joining a lot of clubs they were unable to commit to while children were still dependent. Now the 40–55 year olds are into a variety of projects and trying out skills they had no time for earlier. Expect to add in open houses, elegant sit-down dinners; balls, alumnae weekends, and reunions; museum and gallery showings, card parties, and organized meets for bridge, canasta, dominoes, and pinochle; anything to do with hobbies and creativity like photography, or bird or wildlife identification; computer clubs, decorating parties, investment meetings, book readings, rotaries, volunteering, tutoring, or politics. This age group usually throws showers, engagement parties, weddings; and now there is an increased interest in individual or couples' sports, such as lawn bowling, tennis, racquetball.

55–75 YEARS OLD

Parties with and for children, and their children, take precedence as this group attends grandchildren's recitals, school plays—and frequently participates in family holidays. Gardening, hobbies, and golf are important as well as the people who do them. It is this group's last shot at dancing and a good time to join in for line dancing, ballroom classes, and maybe even tap. People 55–75 feel the need to discover genealogy and renew connections. Computers are timeworthy, and this age group often knows just as much about the Internet and e-mail as the 16–20 year olds; they frequently attend classes on desktop publishing and create newsletters for all the clubs they've joined. There's more casual entertaining, and milestone marker-type events become more popular.

75 AND UP

75-plus agers slow down some, but they still enjoy the teas, dessert parties, and small friendship gatherings they're invited to. Christenings, receptions, and, unfortunately, funerals, will spring up. Reading and discussing books has never before been so interesting or held so much meaning.

APPENDIX H.
WHAT TO DO WHEN–THE COUNTDOWN

4–6 WEEKS BEFORE:

Choose type of party.
Compile guest list.
Decide on invitations and basics like date, time, etc.
Either buy or make cards and buy stamps.
Engage extra help, if necessary.
Make preliminary shopping list.
Assess surroundings and plan basic layouts: prep area, seating, tables, coats, etc.
Choose games and schedule entertainment.

2–4 WEEKS BEFORE:

Issue invitations.
Structure your basic menu along with garnishes and beverages.
Select recipes and tag pages, or copy into book. Set aside.
Compile major grocery list.
Plan flowers and décor.
Check linen supply for cleaning, etc.
Order rentals or other major equipment.
Do major jobs like washing windows, paint touch-ups, lighting.
Do a bar/wine inventory.
Set up music or game accessories.

1 WEEK BEFORE:

Shop for groceries.
Check liquor and soft-drink supplies, pick up.
Begin cleaning and light chore list.
Wash seldom-used dishes and glassware. Polish any silver.
Check basic inventory.
Review facilities list.
Enlist other help or recap with friend.

4 DAYS BEFORE:

Check with any invited guests not heard from.
Double-check layout, and do last-minute purchases.

3 DAYS BEFORE:

Clean your house, apartment, or visit rented facility. Reconfirm location, if entertaining away from home.
Party menu check-up.

Prepare bakery items for freezing.
Work on decorations.
Buy gifts or amenities.

2 DAYS BEFORE:

Save this day for last-minute arrangements and anything you might have overlooked. Check all lists: cleaning, chores, shopping, liquor, stores.
Check outfits for yourself and spouse, or other.
Hairstyle and manicure.
Assemble equipment for all preparation and work areas.
Press linens or other goods.
Prepare any foods that can be done ahead and frozen, refrigerated, or prepared to mix.
Quickie dust and vacuum (major cleaning has been completed).

1 DAY BEFORE:

Set any tables that you can.
Check party-day serving menu.
Chill drinks that don't require ice.
Clean coffee pot.
Bathroom setup.
Prepare fresh ice. Bag, do again.
Reset timers, check lighting.
Double-check entertainment.
Water plants.

DAY OF PARTY:

Prepare food as early in the day as possible. Garnish.
Set up bar, if any. Coffee area too.
Clean up, run dishwasher.
Additional ice purchase if needed. Store.
Fresh flower arrangement.
Freshen bathroom, clean all surfaces.
Lay out clean towels, linens.
Check for ashtrays, candles, odd items, place cards, etc.
Check settings, or buffet.
Check that coatroom is equipped.
Check that bathrooms are equipped.
Last minute touch-ups.
Hang out signs, set up balloon markers or luminaria.

ABOUT THE GUIDE
TO THE GAMES

I have always been loathe to state the amount of time a game takes, because there are so many variables. I usually work a game according to how the players are doing with it. If they're having fun, I milk it. If it's not working out, I ditch it and move on to another rather quickly. The times listed in the following guide therefore are only generalized estimates, meant only to give you a place to start.

Putting an age limit on games is also something I usually avoid. Much depends on the group. But I do want readers to know that games are not just for little kids!

I thought about including a column for preparation, but all games, I believe, require preparation, the least of which is to read through the game several times, put it on an easy-to-read card, and be able to explain it.

As for group size, I feel a few couples make up a dinner event, a small group starts at 10–12 people, adding two or three more pairs is medium size, and anything over that gets large. This, of course, is all relative simply because, over the years, I have worked with clubs, chapter associations, and statewide seminars, so numbers of people do not intimidate me. Go with your comfort level. You can always become the "Game Lady" or "Game Gent" for your area and, who knows? You may even get a reputation as the Party Pro! Whatever your calling, adapt things to make them your own.

GUIDE TO THE GAMES AND INDEX

Name of Game	Page	Type	Number of players	Minutes	YA Child		Adult
Animal Crackers	135	hunt	small group	10	8 up *		*
Area Quiz	83	p/p	small group	15+			*
Back-or-Front Drill	120	skit	small group	20+	*	*	*
Balkan Dodge Ball	108	active	teams	30+	*	*	*
Balloon Anklets	77	get-acq.	pairs	5–10	*	*	*
Balloon Bang	102	relay	teams	10	8 up *		*
Balloon Bomb	109	outdoor	teams	5–10	*	*	*
Balloon Bouquet	150	gift-giving	any	15	*	*	*
Balloon Tennis	103	outdoor	teams	5–10	8 up *		*
Barnyard Competition	114	stunt	any	20+		12 up	*
Big Lucky Letters	135	hunt	small group	20+	*	*	*
Bigamy	111	music	large group	30+	*	*	*
Birthday	87	p/p	small group	10+			*
Blind Postal Clerk	108	active	10–20	10+	*	*	*
Blindfold Cards	96	table	couples	10+			*
Blow It Out	118	forfeit	any	5–10			*
Bombard It	110	active	12	30	*	*	*
Building Matches	73	pre-party	groups of 5/6	10+		*	*
Calling Card	78	get-acq.	any	10–20		*	*
Captain Hook	118	forfeit	any	10+		*	*
Cinderfella	105	relay	teams	10+		*	*
City Tour Highlights	141	event	any	20+	*	*	*
Cobweb Hunt	132	hunt	couples	15+	*	*	*
Consequences	86	p/p	small group	10+			*
Cork in Circle	104	outdoor	teams	20+		*	*
Costume Party	80	defroster	any	20+		*	*
Couple Quiz	77	icebreaker	small group	20+			*
Crazy Airways	141	event	up to 48	30+			*
Creating Ghosts	92	thinking	small group	10+		12 up	*
Crime	137	mystery	any	30+			*
Cushion Touch	109	active	large party	30+	*	*	*
D.I.Y.	68	pre-party	any	15–30	*	*	*
Designers Surprise	125	shower	small group	10+	*	*	*
Dollar Shakedown	78	get-acq.	large group	10–20			*
Estimators	89	p/p	any	10+		*	*
Eternal Triangles	134	hunt	large group	20+		*	*
Family Portrait	145	grouping	any	5–10	*	*	*
Family Reunion	126	shower	small group	5–10+	*	*	*

Name of Game	Page	Type	Number of players	Minutes	Child	YA	Adult
Find Me	144	pairing	any	5–10	*	*	*
Fingerprint Identification	140	mystery	any	20+			*
Five Square	84	p/p	any	20+		*	*
Good Ole Days	84	p/p	any	10+		*	*
Guessing	72	pre-party	any	throughout	8 up	*	*
Guess the Lip Print	140	mystery	any	20+			*
Halves	149	gift-giving	any	15+	*	*	*
Hoops	103	relay	teams	10+	8 up	*	*
Hunt the Pairs	135	hunt	any	20+		*	*
Hunt the Thimble	124	hunt	small group	15+	*	*	*
I Bequeath	116	forfeit	any, helper	10+			*
It's Cold Out	103	relay	teams	10+	8 up	*	*
Jigsaw Puzzle	81	defroster	large group	20+			*
Just Five	124	shower	small group	20+	*	*	*
Last Night	88	p/p	small group	10+			*
Listen	71	pre-party	small group	10–15		12 up	*
Literary Pairs	144	pairing	any	5–10	*	*	*
Map of Treasure Island	68	pre-party	any as guests arrive			*	*
Match It	126	shower	small group	15+		*	*
Matchbox Cram	80	defroster	any	15–20			*
Memory Book	128	shower	small group	30–45	*	*	*
Memory Game	75	get-acq.	any	10–20		*	*
Mostest, The	136	outdoor	pairs	20+			*
Musical Chair Not Removed	112	music	large party	20+	*	*	*
Musical Envelopes	113	music	large party	20+	*	*	*
Musical Groups	114	music	large party	20+	*	*	*
Musical Pack	111	music	any	15–20	*	*	*
Musical Pairs	112	music	large party	20+	*	*	*
Musical Pass	113	music	large party	20+			*
New Business	132	hunt	small group	15+		*	*
Newspaper Couple	120	forfeit	one couple	10+		*	*
Nine Toss	146	tiebreaker	two	5	*	*	*
Object Hunt	80	defroster	large group	15			*
One-Minute Test	121	forfeit	teams	5–20		*	*
One Minute to Go	93	thinking	small group	20+		12 up	*
One-Word Conversation	74	get-acq.	any	10	*	*	*
Only the Best of Friends	125	shower	small group	20+			*
Paper and Hard Evidence	139	mystery	any	30+			*

Name of Game	Page	Type	Number of players	Minutes	Child	YA	Adult
Pass the Package	111	music	any	10+	*	*	*
Passing Beans	101	relay	teams	10+	8 up	*	*
Pea and Spoon	106	relay	teams	10+	*	*	*
Pea Pick	95	table	6–8	5+		*	*
Peanut Carry-on	107	relay	teams	10+	8 up	*	*
Penny Pitching	96	table	small group	20+			*
Personal Favorites	85	p/p	small group	10+			*
Ping-Pong Baseball	110	active	large party	30+		*	*
Plea for the Life Jacket	119	forfeit	small group	10+			*
Polaroid or Digital Camera	131	hunt	small teams	60+			*
Portrait Gallery	82	get-acq.	any	10+		*	*
Postage-Stamp Find	73	pre-party	any	10+		12 up	*
Potato Relay	105	relay	any	20+		12 up	*
Prophecies	95	table	small group	10+		*	*
Quick Switch	70	shower	small group	5–10	*	*	*
Resolutions (New Year's)	96	table	any	15			*
Ringing the Bottle	69	pre-party	small group	3–5		*	*
Rogues Gallery	78	get-acq.	any	20–40		12 up	*
Rose, The	93	table	small group	10+	*	*	*
Rude Remarks	97	thinking	small circle	15+			*
Say It with Two	90	p/p	any	10+			*
Set the Table	85	p/p	any	15+		*	*
Sherlock on the Town	92	p/p	any	10+			*
Similes	143	pairing	any	5–10	*	*	*
Smell Test	71	pre-party	small group	10–20		12 up	*
Something Odd	76	icebreaker	large mixer	15–30	*	*	*
Speech Class	98	thinking	small group	20			*
Statue Love	70	skit	small group	10			*
Steal-a-Gift 2	150	gift-giving	small group	20+	*	*	*
Subway Jam	105	relay	2 teams	5+		12 up	*
Sweet Spoon	106	relay	teams	10+	*	*	*
Table Wares	94	table	any	20+		*	*
Teach a Task	129	activity	small group	30+		12 up	*
There's a Sucker Born Every Minuted	117	forfeit	any	30+			*
Thread on Your Jacket	117	stunt	several actors throughout				*
Tissue Tournament	75	icebreaker	any, teams	10+	*	*	*
Tongue Twisters	119	forfeit	any	5–10	*	*	*

Name of Game	Page	Type	Number of players	Minutes	Child	YA	Adult
Treasure Hunt	133	hunt	large party	20+		*	*
Treasure Hunt 2	134	hunt	large party	20+		*	*
Unique Find-a-Gift	147	gift-giving	small group	20+	*	*	*
Vanity Table	123	shower	small group	10+	*	*	*
Wait a Minute	94	table	4–6	15+	*	*	*
What Do You Hear?	139	mystery	any	20+			*
What Do You Know?	88	p/p	teams	30+			*
What Fabric Is This?	139	mystery	any	20+			*
White Elephant	147	gift-giving	any	30	*	*	*
Who Am I Tonight?	79	get-acq.	large group	15–20		*	*
Who Is This?	79	get-acq.	any	10–15		*	*
Whose Gift?	148	gift-giving	any	30+	*	*	*
Whose Nose?	90	guessing	small	15–30		*	*
Word Association	89	p/p	small group	20+			*
Your Task	115	forfeit	one	10+			*

Author Note

I would love to hear from you . . .

If you have any comments, questions, or would just like to tell me about your party or event, write to me at my web site. The URL is:

http://www.andreacampbell.com